Mrs. Lee's Stories About
Jesus

Mrs. Irven Lee

Illustrated by
Mrs. Bennie Lee Fudge

truth
BOOKS

ISBN 10: 1-58427-392-5

ISBN 13: 978-158427-392-9

Guardian of Truth Foundation
CEI Bookstore
220 S. Marion St., Athens, AL 35611
1-855-49-BOOKS or 1-855-492-6657
www.CEIbooks.com

Jesus Came to Earth

(John 1:1-14)

God lives up in heaven. He looks down on the earth and sees people day and night. He made the world and everything in it.

Jesus is God's Son, and he lives in heaven with God. The Holy Spirit and the angels live in heaven, too.

If we are good and always do the things that God wants us to do, he has promised to take us to heaven to live with him when we die.

God used to talk to people just as we talk to one another, but he does not talk to us that way now. We have

his words written down in the book that we call the Bible.

When we read the Bible, we are listening to God talk to us. When we do the things we are told to do in the Bible, we are obeying God.

We must obey God if we are to be good and get to live with him when we die.

Jesus was with God in the very beginning, and together they made everything.

One time Jesus left heaven and came down to earth and lived here just as we do. He came as a tiny baby just as all of us are born to our mothers.

Jesus grew up like other boys and girls. He wanted to know just how people act and feel so he would understand all about them.

He went back to heaven to live. When we pray to God, Jesus hears our prayers. He tells God about how we feel, because he knows all about us.

I'm going to tell you the story about when he came to earth to live. Before I tell you about Jesus' coming though, I want to tell you about another man who came to tell the people to get ready for Jesus. His name was John.

For a long, long time God had been promising to send his Son to the world who would show the people how to be saved from their sins. Sins are the things we do that are wrong.

Every time a little boy baby was born, I guess the mother would hope that he would grow up to be the one God had promised to send.

The people were expecting Jesus to come, and yet they were not ready for him.

God sent John first to tell the people how to get ready for him.

You will like the story about when John was born.

QUESTIONS

1. Where does God live?
2. Can he see the people on the earth?
3. Who else lives in heaven besides God?
4. What has God promised us if we live the way he has told us?
5. How do we know what God wants us to do?
6. When Jesus came down from heaven to the earth did he come as a little baby?
7. When we pray to God does Jesus hear us and know how we feel?
8. Why did God send Jesus to the earth?
9. Did God send somebody before Jesus to get the people ready?
10. What was the name of the man who came to get the people ready?

The Birth of John
(Luke 1:5-25, 57-80)

In those days the people did not worship God as we do now. They had to go to a place called the Temple to worship.

They had men, called priests, who went into the Temple and burned incense on a little altar while the people outside were praying.

Incense is a kind of gum or spice which smells very sweet when it is burned. The priests burned the incense every morning and every afternoon.

There was an old priest named Zacharias. His wife's name was Elisabeth. They had no children. They were so old that they thought they could never have any children. They were very good and loved God. They had wanted a little boy and had prayed for one.

One day Zacharias was in the Temple burning incense while all the people were praying outside.

All at once Zacharias looked up and saw an angel standing on the right side of the altar where he was burning the incense. He was afraid and did not know what to do.

The angel told him not to be afraid because he had come to tell him some good news.

Angels do not come to people today because we have the Bible to tell us everything that God wants us to know.

It was really good news that this angel, whose name was Gabriel, told Zacharias. He said, "Your wife, Elisabeth, is going to have a little boy. You shall call his name John." It would be

John who would get the people ready for Jesus.

Zacharias could not believe what he heard. He was so old and Elisabeth was so old.

Zacharias said, "How can I know this?" The angel said, "I am Gabriel that stand in the presence of God. I was sent to speak to thee."

Zacharias should have believed it just because an angel told him. God had sent the angel, and that was enough.

The angel told him that because he did not believe what he told him he would be punished by not being able to talk any more until after the child was born.

The people outside began to wonder why Zacharias stayed so long in the Temple.

When he came out he could not talk. He just made signs with his hands. They guessed that he had seen an angel, but they did not know what the angel had told him.

A little while after this Elisabeth had a little baby boy. All their friends and kinsfolk came to see him, and they all wanted to name him.

They wanted to name him Zacharias for his father, but Elisabeth said, "No, he shall be called John."

They wondered why she wanted to name him John because none of their kinsfolk was named John. They did not know that the angel had told them what to name him.

Zacharias still could not talk, so he wrote on a paper, "His name is John." When he wrote that, his mouth was opened so he could talk again. He praised God for giving them the little child.

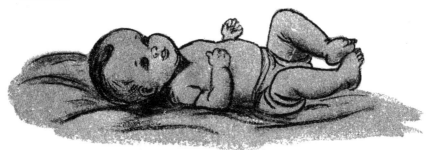

QUESTIONS

1. Where did people used to go to worship God?
2. When Zacharias was in the Temple burning incense what did he see standing by the altar?

3. How did he feel?
4. What did the angel tell him?
5. Did he believe what the angel said?
6. Why did he think he and his wife could not have a little baby boy?
7. How did the angel punish Zacharias for not believing what he said?
8. Did Zacharias and Elisabeth have a little baby boy?
9. What did they name him?
10. Was this the one God promised to send to get the people ready for Jesus?

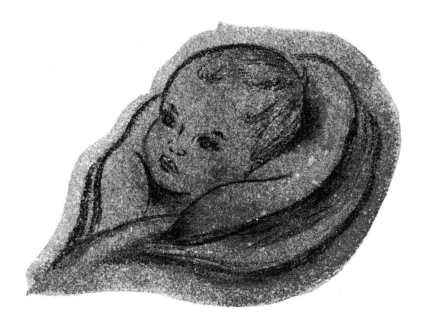

The Birth of Jesus

(Luke 2:1-7)

In a small town called Nazareth there lived a young woman named Mary. She was a real good woman and loved God.

One day the angel Gabriel, the same angel that Zacharias saw in the Temple, went to tell her some good news.

When she saw him she was afraid. She did not know why he had come to see her. He told her not to be afraid. He told her that she was going to have a little baby boy. His name was to be Jesus. He would be called the Son of God. He would be the one whom God had promised to send to the world to save people from their sins.

16

Mary was happy because she was going to be the mother of the Son of God. She was not married when the angel told her this good news, but after a little while she married a man named Joseph.

The king sent out word that all the people must be taxed. They had to go to be taxed back to the town where their fathers and grandfathers used to live.

Joseph and Mary had to leave Nazareth where they were living and go to another town called Bethlehem.

Lots of other people had gone to Bethlehem. All the hotels, or inns as they were called then, were filled.

There was no more room for anybody to spend the night.

When Joseph and Mary got there they could not find a house where they could stay. They had to go to a place where the donkeys stayed. That was not a good place to spend the night, but Joseph and Mary did not complain about it.

That night a wonderful thing happened. The little baby boy that the angel had promised to Mary was born.

Mary did not have any nice, soft bed to put him in. She wrapped him in bands and cloth and laid him in the manger, the trough where the donkeys ate their food. That was not a good bed for the Son of God, was it?

This little child who had to sleep in a manger was the Son of God. God had promised a long time before that he would send his Son into the world, and now he had come just as a tiny baby.

Mary called him Jesus because that was the name the angel had told her to call him.

The name Jesus means Saviour. Jesus came to save people from their sins and to keep them from having to be punished for their sins.

QUESTIONS

1. What did the angel Gabriel tell Mary?
2. What was she to name her little boy?
3. Was this baby boy to be the Son of God?
4. Was Mary happy to be the mother of the Son of God?
5. Whom did Mary marry?
6. When Mary and Joseph went to Bethlehem to be taxed were there lots of other people there so that all the houses were filled?
7. Where did they have to spend the night?
8. What wonderful thing happened that night?
9. What did they name the little baby?
10. Where did Mary put the little baby to sleep?
11. Why did Jesus come down to earth?

The Angels and the Shepherds
(Luke 2:8-20)

On the very night that Jesus was born, there were some shepherds out in the fields watching their sheep.

They could not leave the sheep alone even at night, for some wild animal might kill them.

While they were watching the sheep, all at once they saw an angel standing by them. They were afraid just as Mary and Zacharias were when they saw the angel.

The angel said to them, "Do not be afraid. I have come to tell you some good news." He told them that a Saviour had been born that very night in Bethlehem.

Suddenly there came down from heaven a whole group of angels. They

sang songs and praised God for sending Jesus to the world.

When the angels were gone back to heaven, the shepherds said to each other, "Let us go to Bethlehem and see the child."

They went and found Joseph and Mary. They found the baby Jesus lying in the manger. They thanked God for sending his Son down to earth. They were happy when they went back to their sheep.

QUESTIONS

1. Why did the shepherds have to stay with their sheep at night?
2. Whom did they see standing by them?
3. Had the angel come to tell them good news?
4. What did he tell them?
5. When the angels had gone away where did the shepherds go?
6. Did they thank God for sending his Son to the world?

The Visit of the Wise Men
(Matt. 2)

There were some wise men in the East who were watching the stars.

One night a new and strange star appeared in the sky. It was a star that had been put in the sky to lead the men to the place where Jesus was.

The wise men followed the star until they got to Jerusalem. They stopped there and began to ask where the child was who had been born to be the "king of the Jews."

When Herod, the king who lived in Jerusalem, heard that there had been a new king born, he was scared.

He was afraid somebody else would get to be king in his place. He called the wise men to him and asked them all about the baby king.

Herod told the wise men to go and find the baby and come back and tell him. He said he wanted to go and worship him too.

That was not what Herod wanted to do. He wanted to find out where Jesus was so that he could have him killed.

The wise men left Jerusalem and started toward Bethlehem.

The star that had been leading them on the way went before them again. It led them right to the house where Jesus was.

When they saw him, they fell on their knees and worshipped him. They gave him nice presents to show how glad they were that he was born.

When they started to go home, they were told by God in a dream not to go back through Jerusalem where Herod lived because he was wanting to kill Jesus. They went home another way.

When Herod found out that the wise men had gone home another way and had not minded him, he was very, very angry. He was so angry that he decided he would just kill all the little boy babies. He thought sure he would kill Jesus, too. He did not know that God was taking care of Jesus. He killed lots and lots of babies, but he did not kill Jesus.

Just as soon as the wise men had gone home, an angel came to Joseph while he was asleep. The angel told Joseph to get up quickly, take Mary and Jesus, and go away to another country called Egypt.

When Herod was killing all the little babies in Bethlehem, Jesus was far away down in Egypt. God was taking care of him, so Herod could not hurt him.

Joseph, Mary, and Jesus stayed in Egypt until an angel came and told Joseph that the wicked king Herod was dead.

They started to go back to Bethlehem where Jesus was born, but they heard that Herod's son was king, and they were afraid.

God spoke to Joseph in a dream and told him to go to Nazareth to live.

QUESTIONS

1. Why did God put a new star in the sky when Jesus was born?
2. When the wise men got to Jerusalem whom did they ask about Jesus?
3. Why was Herod scared when he heard that a new king was born?
4. Did he tell the wise men to find Jesus and come tell him where he was so he could go and worship him?
5. Did he really want to worship him?
6. When the wise men found Jesus what did they do to show how glad they were that he was born?
7. When they started home did God tell them to go another way and not see Herod?
8. Was Herod very angry?
9. What did he do to all the little boy babies he could find?
10. Did he kill Jesus?
11. Where had Joseph taken Mary and Jesus?
12. Who was taking care of Jesus?

Jesus in the Temple

(Luke 2:21-52)

Every year Joseph and Mary went up to Jerusalem to keep a feast. God had told them to go and worship him that way.

When Jesus was twelve years old, he went with them to the feast.

The people in those days did not have good ways to travel as we do now. They had to walk or go on donkeys and camels. When they made the long trip to

Jerusalem, they went in groups so they could protect themselves from robbers along the way.

Joseph and Mary and the group they had gone with stayed until the feast was over. Then they started home.

They supposed that Jesus was with them, but when they stopped to spend the night they discovered he was not there. They were very worried.

Joseph and Mary went back to Jerusalem to look for him. They looked through the whole city for three days.

Finally they found him in the Temple. That was God's house where the people went to worship.

Jesus was with the leaders and teachers asking and answering questions. They were all surprised at the things he knew.

Mary asked him why he had treated them that way. She and Joseph had been very sad while they were looking for him.

Jesus asked, "Why did you look for me? Did you not know I must be about my Father's business?"

His father was God, but Joseph and Mary did not understand what he meant.

Jesus went home with them to Nazareth. He grew up there and obeyed them just as all boys and girls should obey their parents.

QUESTIONS

1. How old was Jesus when he went with Mary and Joseph to keep the feast?
2. Did the people go in groups to protect themselves from robbers?
3. When the group started home was Jesus with them?

4. When Mary and Joseph saw that Jesus was not with them, were they worried?
5. When they started back to look for him, how long did it take them to find him?
6. Where was he?
7. What was he doing?
8. What did he tell them?
9. Who was his Father?
10. Did he go home with them and obey them as boys and girls must obey their parents now?

Jesus is Baptized

(Matt. 3)

John, whom I have already told you about, grew up to be a man and lived out in the wilderness. The wilderness was a place where very few people lived. John was alone most of the time.

He began to preach to the people who came out from Jerusalem and all the other places round about.

He told them that Jesus was coming soon to save them from their sins. He had been sent to tell them how to be ready for him.

John told them to stop doing the things that were wrong and do good to everybody. He told them to be baptized and show that they were ready to receive Jesus.

John baptized all the people who believed his teaching in a river called the Jordan River.

Because he baptized people and probably because he was the first preacher to baptize people, he was called John the Baptist.

When Jesus was thirty years old, he left his home in Nazareth. He walked a long, long way to the Jordan River where John was preaching and baptizing people.

He told John that he wanted to be

baptized. John did not want to baptize him because he knew he was such a good man.

John said, "I ought to let you baptize me." Jesus told him to do it because he wanted to do everything God wanted him to do. John baptized him.

When they came up out of the water, the Spirit of God came down from heaven, and it looked like a dove. It sat on Jesus' head. A voice came from heaven saying, "This is my beloved Son, in whom I am well pleased."

God was pleased with Jesus for doing what he wanted him to do. He is pleased with us when we do the things he wants us to do.

QUESTIONS

1. Where did John live?
2. What did he tell the people about Jesus?
3. What did he say the people must do to get ready for Jesus?
4. Why did people call him John the Baptist?
5. How old was Jesus when he came to be baptized?
6. Did John want to baptize him?
7. What did John say Jesus ought to do?
8. Was Jesus baptized because God wanted him to be?
9. When he was baptized and came up out of the water what came and sat on his head?
10. What did God say?

John Is Killed

(Matt. 14:1-12)

The king who lived then was a very wicked man. His wife was a very wicked woman.

John the Baptist told them that they were doing wrong. It made them mad, so they had John put in prison.

One day the king gave a big dinner to some of his people. They were drinking wine and doing lots of things that are not right.

A girl came in and danced before the king. He liked the dancing, and he told her he would give her anything she wanted.

She did not know what to ask for, so she went and asked her mother. Her mother was the king's wife. She hated

John because he told them they were not living as God wanted them to. She told the girl to ask the king to give her John's head.

I do not think that was a very good present.

The king was sorry. He had put

John in prison, but he did not want to kill him. He had told the girl he would give her anything she asked for, so he sent some men to the prison and had John's head cut off.

He gave it to the girl, and she carried it to her mother. When John's friends heard about it, they were very sad. They went and got his body and buried it.

QUESTIONS

1. What did John tell the wicked king and his wife?
2. What did they do to him?
3. When the girl came and danced for the king what did he promise to give her?
4. What did she ask for?
5. What did the king do to John?
6. When John's friends heard about it, what did they do?

Jesus in the Wilderness
(Matt. 4:1-11)

After Jesus had been baptized, Satan came to him and tried to make him do wrong.

Jesus had gone out in the wilderness to talk to God. The wilderness was a place where nobody lived, so he was out there alone.

He stayed forty days and forty nights and did not have anything to eat. He was very, very hungry.

Satan came to him and said, "If you are the Son of God make these stones into bread."

You remember that God had said that Jesus was his Son when he was baptized. Satan tried to get him to prove that he was the Son of God. It would have been wrong for Jesus to do something that God had not told him to do, so he would not turn the stones into bread.

He said that man could not live by bread alone, but he had to listen to God's words.

Satan then took him up on top of the Temple, God's house. He told him if he was the son of God to jump off and see if the angels would catch him.

Jesus would not mind him. God had promised to take care of Jesus, but he would not do it if he were doing what Satan told him to do.

Satan then took Jesus up on a real high mountain. He showed him all the world and the beautiful things in it. He told him that he would give him everything in it if he would fall down and worship him.

Jesus told Satan he could not do so because God had said that people must not worship anybody but him.

Satan could not make him do anything that was wrong, so he went away and left him. When he was gone away, the angels came down from heaven and gave Jesus food.

QUESTIONS

1. After Jesus was baptized, who came and tried to get him to do wrong?
2. How long did Jesus stay out in the wilderness by himself?
3. Did he eat any food while he was there?
4. What did Satan tell him to do to the stones?
5. Did Jesus do it? Why?
6. When Satan took Jesus on top of the Temple, what did he tell him to do?
7. Would Jesus mind him?
8. Did Satan say he would give Jesus everything in the world if he would worship him?

9. Is it right to worship anybody but God?

10. When Jesus would not mind him, did Satan leave him alone?

11. What did the angels do when Satan left Jesus?

Jesus Turns Water to Wine

(John 2:1-11)

Jesus began to teach the people about God. He told them that he had come to save them from their sins.

Lots of people came to hear him teach. Many of them believed that he was the Son of God, but some of them did not like him.

He picked out twelve men to stay with him all the time and help him teach other people. The twelve men were called apostles.

The apostles believed that Jesus was the Son of God. They liked to talk to him and to listen to him talk about God.

One day there was a wedding in a town called Cana.

In those days when there was a wedding the people made a feast and invited lots of other people to come.

Jesus, his mother, and his disciples were all there.

At the feasts the people drank wine. At this feast there were lots of people, and the wine was all drunk, and the people wanted more.

Jesus' mother came to him and said, "They have no wine."

Jesus said, "What have I to do with thee?" That meant, "What do you want me to do?"

She told the servants to do whatever he told them to do. There were six big pots sitting there that the people used to carry water in.

Jesus said to the servants, "Fill the pots with water."

The servants filled the pots with water and poured it out. When they poured it out, it was not water–it was wine.

Jesus told them to take it and show it to the governor. The governor was the man who had charge of the feast. He was the one who had to see that the people had enough food to eat and enough wine to drink.

The servants carried the wine to him, and the governor tasted it. It was real good, and he said they had saved the best till last.

He did not know that Jesus had made the wine, but the servants knew.

QUESTIONS

1. Did the people like to hear Jesus talk about God?
2. What were the twelve men called whom Jesus picked out to help him teach the people?
3. When Jesus and his disciples went to the wedding, what happened to the wine?
4. What did Jesus' mother do?
5. What did he tell the servants to do?
6. When they started to pour the water out of the jars, what happened to the water?
7. What did the governor say about the wine?
8. Did he know where it came from?

Jesus Teaches and Heals the People

(Matt. 5-8)

Jesus often went up on a mountain or sat on the shore of the sea to teach the crowds of people who came to him.

The people came in crowds because they had never heard anyone else teach as he did.

He taught them to be kind and to love one another. He told them to love not only their friends but also their enemies, the ones that treated them wrong.

He taught them that they must not kill anybody, or take things that did not belong to them, or tell things that were not true about others. They were not even to be angry with other people.

He told his disciples that they were

to be like a city on a hill that could be seen all around. Others would look at them and see that they did as Jesus told them. That would make them want to live right, too.

He told them if someone asked for something, for them to give him much more than he asked for. That is the way God does when we pray to him. He hears and gives us more than we ask for.

Jesus taught many, many things

about God and the things he wanted the people to do.

He did not always teach the people out on the mountain or along the shore of the sea. He went many places. Often he went into the synagogues.

The synagogues were places where the people met to read and study about God. They were about like our church houses. The people would meet to study, and Jesus would preach to them.

One day when he left the synagogue he went home with Peter, one of his disciples.

Peter's wife's mother was sick with a fever.

Jesus went in the room where she was, took her by the hand, and helped her up. When she rose up, she was well. She was very glad, and began to do things for Jesus.

That evening when it was getting late, the people began to bring all the sick people to Peter's home where Jesus was so he could make them well.

He healed all of them, and then the people begged him to stay with them a long time.

He told them that he could not stay long because he had to go to other places and teach other people, too.

There were lots of other sick people that he wanted to make well, and lots of other people he wanted to tell about God, so he could not stay long in one place.

QUESTIONS

1. Where did Jesus often go to teach the people?
2. Why did they like to hear him?
3. Tell some of the things Jesus taught.
4. What was the synagogue?

5. Did Jesus often go and preach in the synagogue?

6. Where did he go one day when he left the synagogues?

7 Whom did he find sick?

8. What did he do to her?

9. Whom did the people bring to him that evening?

10. What did they beg him to do?

11. Why did he say he could not stay a long time with them?

The Great Net of Fishes
(Luke 5:1-11)

All the people wanted to hear Jesus talk about God. They came in great crowds to hear him.

I told you that he often went into the synagogues to talk to them. Sometimes he talked to them out by a lake of water. The name of the lake where he so often taught the people was the lake of Galilee or the Sea of Galilee.

One day he was teaching by the lake of Galilee, and there were so many people they were pushing against him.

He saw two boats sitting there by the edge of the water. One of the boats belonged to Peter.

Jesus got into the boat and told Peter to push it out into the water a

little way so the people could not touch
him. He sat in the boat and told the
people about God and what they must
do to please him.

When he had finished teaching the people he told Peter to put his net down into the water to catch some fish.

Peter and some of the other disciples were fishermen. That means they made their living by catching fish and selling them. They used nets to catch them so they could catch lots at a time.

When Jesus told him to put his net into the water to catch some fish, Peter said, "We have worked hard all night, and we have not caught any fish at all, but since you told me to, I will do it."

He put his net down into the water. So many fish came into it that the net began to break.

Peter called to the men in the other boat to come help him get the fish into his boat. He then fell down before Jesus and worshipped him.

He knew that Jesus had made all the fish come into the net. He was ashamed that he had not wanted to put the net down as soon as Jesus told him to do it.

When the disciples had brought their nets with the fish into the boat, they left them and followed Jesus. They wanted to be with him wherever he went.

QUESTIONS

1. Did lots of people want to hear Jesus talk about God?
2. Where did he often go to teach them?
3. When they pushed against him, did he go into a boat to talk?
4. Whose boat was it?
5. When he was through preaching, what did he tell Peter to do?
6. What did Peter say?
7. When Peter minded Jesus did he catch lots of fish?
8. Did Peter fall down on the ground and worship Jesus?

The Man Sick of the Palsy

(Mk. 2:1-12, LK. 5:18-26)

Jesus went to his own house in a city called Capernaum. All the people around went to see him and hear him preach.

They crowded into the house so that there was no more room even at the doors and windows.

Nobody else could get inside, and people were standing all around the house.

There was a man who was sick with a very bad disease called palsy. He could not walk at all and probably could hardly move himself on his bed.

He had four friends who knew about Jesus. They knew that Jesus could make people well. They wanted him to see Jesus, but he could not walk to the house where he was.

They thought of a way they could help him. They took up the little bed that the man was lying on and carried it with the sick man on it.

They went to Jesus' house but there were so many people around the house they could not even get to the door. They believed that he could make him well if only they could get him in the house by him.

The four friends did not go back home. They thought of a way to get the sick man into the house.

They took the bed up on the top of the house, on the roof. They were not slanting like our houses, or the men could not have stood up when they got up there.

They took up part of the roof until they had made a big hole, big enough for the bed to go through. Then they fastened cords to the bed and let it down through the hole in the roof.

The sick man was seen lying on his bed right in front of Jesus. Jesus saw him and looked up through the hole and saw his four friends. He was happy to see people who believed he could make the sick man well.

Jesus turned to the man in the bed and said, "Arise, take up thy bed, and go into thy house." The man got up, took up his bed, and walked out of the house. He was well again.

Some of the people standing in the house did not like for Jesus to make people well. They said that nobody but God could do these things. They did not like for Jesus to say that he was the Son of God.

Lots of people did believe he was the Son of God though, and they followed him around from place to place to listen to him.

QUESTIONS

1. Why did all the people go to Jesus' house?
2. Was there room for any more people to get into the house?
3. Who came to the house bringing a sick man?
4. How did they bring him?
5. Could they take the sick man into the house?
6. Did they go back home?
7. What did they do?
8. Did they let the sick man down through a hole in the roof?
9. Was Jesus pleased when he saw the men who believed he could make the man well?
10. What did he say to the sick man?
11. What did the sick man do?

12. Were some of the people angry at Jesus for making the man well?
13. Did they like for Jesus to say he was the Son of God?
14. Did some of the people believe that Jesus was the Son of God?
15. Did he teach the people that followed him even when he was hungry and tired?

Jesus Heals on the Sabbath

(Luke 6:6-12)

God's people were called Jews. They did not worship God as we do now. They went to the synagogue on the Sabbath day to worship.

The Sabbath day was the last day of the week, or Saturday. We worship on the first day of the week, or Sunday.

The Jews could not do any work at all on the Sabbath day. They could not even cook or bring in wood or anything like that.

One Sabbath day Jesus went into the synagogue with the people as they went to worship.

In the synagogue was a man whose right hand was withered. It was smaller than his other hand, and he could not use it.

The people watched Jesus to see if he would make the hand well. They wanted him to do it so they could say he had worked on the Sabbath day. They could then say he had done wrong.

The Pharisees were Jews who thought they were real good, but Jesus knew that they were not.

They did not like Jesus because he told them they did things that were wrong. They wanted to kill him, so they watched him all the time trying to find something wrong with him.

Jesus looked around at all the people. He knew what the Pharisees were thinking.

He told the man that had the withered hand to stand up where everybody could see him. Then he turned to the Pharisees and said, "Is it right to do good on the Sabbath day or to do evil?"

He asked them if one of their sheep should fall into a pit on the Sabbath day would they pull it out. They knew that they would do that.

Jesus said to the man, "Stretch out your hand." He stretched it out, and it was as large and as strong as the other one.

That made the Pharisees very, very angry. They went out and got with some more wicked people, called the Herodians, and they planned how they could destroy Jesus.

When Jesus knew what they had done, he left that place and went into a mountain by himself. He prayed to God all night.

QUESTIONS

1. Which day of the week did the Jews worship God?
2. Which day do we worship him?
3. Were the Jews supposed to do any work on the Sabbath day?
4. When Jesus went to the synagogue whom did he see there who needed to be healed?
5. Why did the people watch Jesus?
6. Did the Pharisees want him to heal the man so they could say he had done wrong?
7. What did Jesus ask the Pharisees?
8. What did he tell the man with the withered hand?
9. What did the man do?

10. When the Pharisees saw it what did they do?

11. Did Jesus leave when he heard what the Pharisees had done?

12. Where did he go?

Jesus Raises a Man from the Dead
(Luke 7:11-16)

Jesus and his disciples started into a city called Nain.

Lots of people were following him to hear him talk and to see him heal people.

When they got to the gate of the city they saw a crowd of people coming out. The men in front were carrying a coffin that had a dead man in it.

The dead man was the only son of a woman who was a widow. That means her husband was dead, too.

The woman was crying because her son was dead. Lots of people from the city were with her, and they were crying, too.

When Jesus saw them, he was very sorry for the woman. He told the men who were carrying the dead man to stand still.

They stopped, and he said to the dead man, "Young man, I say unto you, Arise."

The young man got up and began to talk. Jesus gave him back to his mother alive and well again.

When all the people saw that Jesus could even bring the dead to life again, they wondered what kind of man he was. They said he was a prophet.

A prophet was a man sent by God to tell the people when they were doing wrong and what to do to please God again.

Jesus was a prophet in that God had sent him, but he was more than a prophet. He was the Son of God.

He made sick people well and made dead people alive to make people believe that he was the Son of God.

He came to live in the world so he could teach everybody how to live right. He wants us to do the things that he tells us to do so that we will not have to be punished for our sins, but that we may get to live with him in heaven when we die.

QUESTIONS

1. When Jesus and his disciples started into the city whom did they see coming out?
2. What were the men in front carrying?
3. Was the dead man the only son of his mother?
4. Was Jesus sorry for the woman?
5. What did he tell the men to do?
6. What did he say to the dead man?
7. What did the dead man do?
8. Who did the people say Jesus was?

9. Whose Son is Jesus?

10. Why did he make sick people well and make dead people come back to life?

11. Why does he want us to do what he tells us to do?

A Great Storm
(Luke 8:22-25)

Jesus had been teaching the people all day by the sea of Galilee. When evening came he sent the crowd of people away because he was very tired.

He got into a boat with his disciples and said, "Let us go across the lake to the other side." They started, and Jesus was so tired he lay down in the back of the boat and went to sleep.

After a little while a great storm came up. The wind blew so hard that the boat was nearly blown to pieces. The water washed up on the sides and into it. The boat was about to sink.

When the disciples saw that the boat was filling with water they became frightened. They thought that they would be drowned.

They saw that Jesus was asleep in the back of the boat. They thought he did not know anything about the storm.

They waked him saying, "Carest thou not that we perish?" That meant, "Don't you care if we are drowned?"

Jesus got up. He said to his disciples, "Why are you afraid?"

He was not afraid, and they should not have been afraid when he was with them.

He said to the wind, "Peace, be still." The wind stopped blowing, and the water became still and smooth again.

The boat could sail without any water blowing into it.

The disciples were surprised again to see what wonderful things Jesus could do. They said to each other, "What kind of a man is this that even the wind and the sea obey him?"

The disciples had seen Jesus change water into wine, heal sick people, and make a dead man alive again.

Now they had seen him make the wind stop blowing.

They wondered what kind of man he was because they had never seen anyone like him before.

Jesus did those things to make his disciples and all the people who followed him believe that he was the Son of God.

QUESTIONS

1. Where did Jesus go after he had sent the people away?
2. When he got into the boat what did he do?
3. Did a bad storm come up?
4. How did the disciples feel?
5. Why were they frightened?
6. When they saw that Jesus was asleep, what did they do?

7. What did Jesus ask them?
8. What did he say to the wind?
9. What did the wind and water do?
10. What did the disciples say to each other?
11. What else had they seen Jesus do?
12. Why did Jesus do these wonderful things?

The Man with an Unclean Spirit
(Luke 8:26-40)

When Jesus and his disciples had crossed the sea of Galilee, after he had made the wind stop blowing, they came to the country of the Gadarenes.

When he came out of the boat a man came to meet him and worshipped him.

The man had an unclean spirit. In those days the devil could send unclean spirits into people and make them sick or sometimes make them do wicked things. These unclean spirits were called demons.

Nobody could make a man well who had the demons except Jesus or one of Jesus' disciples when Jesus told him to.

The man who came out to the boat to meet Jesus was a very wild man. The demon or unclean spirit in him made him do things he did not want to do.

This man lived out in the tombs where dead people were buried. He was so wild and fierce that nobody could pass by the place.

Men had tried to tie him with ropes and chains, but he would break them and be wild again. He wore no clothes. He stayed in the tombs in the mountains all day and all night, crying and cutting himself with stones.

When he saw Jesus he did not try to hurt him. He fell down on the ground and worshipped him. He called him the Son of God.

The demons knew Jesus. Jesus was sorry for the man and said to the demons, "Come out of the man, thou unclean spirit."

He asked the demons their name, and they said, "Legion, for we are many." Legion means many, and there were lots of them in the man. The demons did not want Jesus to make them go out of the man.

There was a big herd of swine, or hogs, in a field close by. The demons asked Jesus to let them go into the swine. He told them to go. They came out of the man and went into the swine.

The swine or hogs ran down the side of the mountain and were drowned in the water in the sea.

When the men who were taking care of the swine saw what had happened, they were frightened. They ran to tell everybody they saw what had happened.

The people all rushed out to see Jesus. When they got there they saw

Jesus, his disciples, and the man who had had the demons. The man had on his clothes and was just like the other men.

The people wondered who Jesus was and how he could do those things. They were so frightened over the things that had happened that they begged Jesus to leave their country.

Jesus got into the boat with his disciples and started to leave.

The man who was healed came and asked Jesus to let him go with him. He was not afraid of him. He was so happy to be well that he just wanted to stay always with him. Jesus told him to go home to his friends and tell them the great thing that had been done to him.

The man left and went through all his country telling everybody about Jesus and how he had made him well.

Jesus went back across the sea in the boat with his disciples. When he got to the other side he found a great crowd of people waiting for him.

QUESTIONS

1. Who came to meet Jesus when he came out of the boat?
2. What was the matter with the man?
3. Where did he live?

4. How did he act?
5. What did he do when he saw Jesus?
6. What did he call Jesus?
7. When Jesus told the demons to come out where did they want to go?
8. What did the swine do?
9. What did the men do who were taking care of the swine?
10. What did the people of the country beg Jesus to do?
11. What did the man ask Jesus to let him do?
12. What did Jesus tell him to do?
13. What did the man then do?
14. When Jesus got to the other side of the sea, whom did he find?

Jesus Raises a Girl from the Dead

(Matt. 9:18-26)

I have told you about the synagogues, the places where the Jews met to study and worship.

There was a man who had charge of each synagogue and looked after the services. He was called the ruler of the synagogue.

There was a ruler named Jairus. He had only one little girl. She was twelve years old. The little girl became very sick and was about to die.

Jairus had heard about all the wonderful things Jesus could do. He could stop a storm just by speaking to the wind. He could make a man get up out of bed and walk when he had been sick for a long time. He could do many other wonderful things that we call miracles.

Jairus thought if Jesus could come to see his daughter he could make her well. He went out to find Jesus.

When he found him he fell down on the ground and worshipped him. He told him that his little girl was dying and asked him to come and heal her. Jesus started with the ruler of the synagogue. A great crowd of people went with him.

Before they reached the house where the little girl was, some one came out of the house and said to the ruler, "Your daughter is dead. Do not trouble the master any longer."

When Jesus heard that, he said to Jairus, "Do not be afraid, believe on me, and she will be made well."

They came to the house. Jesus would not let any of the people go into the house with him except Peter, James, and John.

There was a crowd of people in the house crying because the little girl was dead.

Jesus said to them, "Do not cry. She is not dead. She is asleep."

The people laughed at him because they knew she was dead. He meant

that she would not be dead long, but it would be just as if she were asleep.

He put all out of the room except Peter, James, John, and the father and mother of the girl.

He went to the bed where the child was lying, took her by the hand and said to her, "Arise."

She opened her eyes and got up.

Jesus told her father and mother to give her something to eat. They were all surprised and wondered at such a thing being done.

Jesus told them not to tell anybody what had happened because such crowds of people were already following him that he did not have time to eat or rest.

QUESTIONS

1. What was the name of the ruler of the synagogue?
2. Was his little girl very sick?

3. What did he think Jesus could do if he could see the little girl?

4. Before they reached the house, what did some one come and tell Jairus?

5. What did Jesus say?

6. When they came to the house, whom did Jesus take in with him?

7. What did he tell the people in the house?

8. Why did they laugh at him?

9. What did he mean?

10. Whom did he take with him into the room where the girl was?

11. What did he say to the little girl?

12. What did she do?

13. What did he tell her father and mother to give her?

14. Did Jesus want them to tell what he had done?

15. Why did he not want them to tell it?

A Sick Woman Is Made Well
(Luke 8:41-42, 49-56)

When Jesus was on his way to the home of Jairus, the ruler of the synagogue, a great crowd followed him. They pressed against him as he walked.

There came a woman into the crowd who had been sick for twelve years. She had spent all of her money trying to get well, but none of the doctors could help her.

She said to herself, "If I can touch even Jesus' clothes, I will be well."

She pushed her way through the crowd and touched his clothes. Just as she touched him she was well.

Jesus stopped, turned around, and said, "Who touched me?"

He felt some one touch him and

knew that power had gone out of his body to heal her.

One of the disciples said, "Why do you ask who touched you? All the people are pressing you."

Jesus said again, "Who touched me?"

The woman came up to him trembling. She told him that she had touched him. She told him that she had been sick for twelve years and could not get well. She thought if she could just touch him she would get well, and that was true.

Jesus told her not to worry any more because her faith had made her well. That meant that she had believed he could do it, and that was the reason she was well.

Jesus liked to find people who believed he could do miracles. He wanted them to believe the things he did and the things he told them.

He wants us now to believe the things the Bible tells us about him. He wants us to do the things he tells us to do.

QUESTIONS

1. When the crowd was following Jesus, who pushed through the crowd to touch him?
2. How long had she been sick?
3. Had she spent all her money trying to get well?
1. Could the doctors make her well?
5. What did she say to herself?
6. When she touched Jesus, what happened?
7. What did Jesus say?
8. What did the disciples say to him?
9. What did he say again?
10. What did the woman do when she came to him?
11. What did Jesus tell her?
12. Does Jesus like for people to believe what he says and do what he says do?

Five Loaves of Bread and Two Fishes

(Matt. 14:13-23)

Jesus carried his disciples out into a desert place, or a place where nobody lived, so they could rest a while.

A great crowd of people saw them going away and ran after them.

When Jesus saw the crowd he was sorry for them.

He said they looked like sheep that had no shepherd.

He began to teach them and to heal all the sick people that they brought to him. He taught them until it was late in the evening.

The disciples came to Jesus and said, "Send the people away because they have been here all day without any food and are very hungry. Tell them to go

away into the towns where they can buy food."

Jesus said, "They do not need to go away. You give them something to eat."

The disciples answered, "We have only five loaves of bread and two small fishes. What would that be among so many people?" Now, there were about five thousand people.

Jesus said, "Bring me the loaves and the fishes."

They brought them to him. He said, "Make the people all sit down on the grass."

When the people had all sat down on the grass, Jesus took the five loaves and the two fishes. He looked up to heaven and gave thanks to God for them. He gave them to the disciples. The disciples gave them to the people.

The loaves and the fishes became more and more until there was plenty for all.

The crowd of people ate all they wanted, and there was still some food left.

Jesus said to his disciples, "Take up all that is left so that nothing will be lost."

They gathered up all that was left. There were twelve baskets full. When the people all saw what was done, they said, "This is truly that prophet that should come into the world."

Jesus was a prophet, but he was much more than a prophet. He is the Son of God.

Jesus then told his disciples to get into a boat and go across the lake while he sent the people away.

When the people had gone, he went up into a mountain alone and prayed. He stayed nearly all night there talking to God.

QUESTIONS

1. Why did Jesus take his disciples into a desert place?
2. What did the crowd of people do when they saw Jesus and his disciples going?
3. Why was Jesus sorry for the people?
4. How long did he teach them?
5. What did the disciples tell Jesus to do?
6. What did Jesus tell them to do?
7. How much food did they have?
8. What did the disciples tell the people to do?

9. When Jesus took the five loaves and two fishes, what did he do?
10. How many people were there?
11. Did the loaves and fishes become more and more so that everybody had plenty to eat?
12. How much was left over?
13. Who did the people say Jesus was?
14. Who is Jesus?
15. Where did Jesus go when he sent the people away?

The Wind and the Sea Obey Jesus
(Matt. 14:24-33)

The disciples of Jesus had gone into a boat and started across the sea of Galilee after Jesus had fed the five thousand people.

Jesus was alone up in the mountain praying. It was night.

A great storm came up so that the disciples could not row their little boat across the water.

The wind and the water tossed the boat about so that the disciples were very afraid. They worked nearly all night trying to keep the boat from sinking.

Early in the morning before it was daylight, Jesus saw the disciples. He knew they were afraid.

He started to them walking on the water.

The disciples saw him coming and thought he was a spirit. They cried out because they were so afraid. Jesus said, "It is I. Be not afraid."

Peter said, "Lord, if it is you, tell me to come to you walking on the water."

Jesus answered, "Come."

Peter stepped out of the boat and started toward Jesus. He was walking on the water. He looked around and saw how the wind was tossing the water all around him, and he became afraid. He began to sink and cried out to Jesus, "Save me."

Jesus put out his hand and touched him. He told him that he did not believe on him as he should or he would not be afraid.

Jesus and Peter went into the boat and the wind stopped blowing. The water became still and smooth again. All at once the disciples in their little boat were at the other side of the lake where they were going.

They were surprised because of what had happened. They had just seen Jesus feed five thousand people with only five loaves and two small fishes. He had walked on the water, let Peter walk on the water, and stopped a storm. Once before they had seen him stop a storm.

They fell down on their knees and worshipped him. They said, "Of a truth thou art the Son of God."

That was what Jesus wanted them to believe. He did all those wonderful things so that they would believe that he was the Son of God.

QUESTIONS

1. What happened while the disciples were in the boat?
2. Was Jesus with them?
3. Where was he?
4. How long did the disciples work trying to

keep the little boat from sinking?

5. When Jesus saw the disciples, how did he go to them?

6. When they saw him coming what did they think he was?

7. What did Jesus say?

8. What did Peter say?

9. What did Jesus tell Peter?

10. When Peter saw the wind blowing so hard what did he do?

11. When Jesus came into the boat what happened?

12. How did the disciples feel?

13. Who did they say Jesus was?

14. Why did Jesus do those wonderful things?

A Gentile Woman's Daughter Is Healed

(Mark 7:24-30, Matt. 15:21-31)

I have told you that God's people were called Jews.

All other people were called Gentiles.

Any Gentile could become a Jew if he wanted to. In that way he could become one of God's people.

The Jews did not like the Gentiles. They would not eat with them, or even stay close to them if they could help it. They treated the Gentiles like dogs and often called them dogs.

Jesus came to show people that one man is as good as another in God's sight. All men can be pleasing to him if they will obey him.

Jesus and his disciples went into a place called Sidon.

They went into a house. They did not want people to know that they were there, but they could not keep them from knowing it.

As soon as the people knew Jesus was in the house they came to him in great crowds to listen to him and see him heal sick people.

A Gentile woman came into the crowd and cried to Jesus to help her.

Jesus at first did not seem to notice her. The disciples asked him to send her away because she bothered them.

Jesus looked at her and asked her what she wanted.

She fell down on her knees and worshipped him. She said, "My daughter has a demon. I want you to heal her."

Demons were wicked spirits that

Satan sent into people. Nobody could make them leave except Jesus.

Jesus said to the woman, "It is not good to take the children's bread and give it to the dogs."

He called the Jews "children" and the Gentiles "dogs" just as the Jews did. He wanted to see what the woman would say.

She said, "That is true, Lord, but even the dogs eat of the crumbs that fall from the children's table."

When Jesus heard that, he was very glad.

She had believed he could heal her daughter, and she was just waiting for him to do it.

Jesus said to her, "Great is your faith. Your daughter will be well."

He made her well because the woman believed in him so much.

Jesus went up on a mountain and sat down. The people came to him bringing all their sick, their crippled, and their blind friends, and he healed them all.

The people wondered at the things they saw. They thanked God for sending Jesus to them.

We should thank God often for sending Jesus to the world.

If Jesus had not come we could not be forgiven of our sins.

Since he came and taught us how to live, we can obey him and get to live in heaven with him when we die.

QUESTIONS

1. What were God's people called?
2. What were all other people called?
3. What did the Jews call the Gentiles?
4. When the Gentile woman came to Jesus, what did she want him to do?

5. What did Jesus say to her?
6. What did she say?
7. Why did Jesus heal her daughter?
8. Where did Jesus go when he left her?
9. Why did the people thank God?
10. Why should we thank him now?

The Good Confession

(Matt. 16:13-20)

Jesus and his disciples went into the country of Caesarea Philippi. As they went Jesus asked them saying, "Who do men say that I am?"

The disciples answered, "Some say you are John the Baptist. Others say you are one of the prophets."

People thought that John the Baptist or one of the prophets had come back alive.

Jesus said then to his disciples, "Who do you say that I am?"

Peter answered, "Thou art the Christ, the Son of the living God."

Jesus was glad that Peter had said that. Jesus blessed him.

He began to tell them that because he was the Son of God he was going to build his church. Nothing would keep him from it.

He told them that he would have to be killed first, but even being killed would not keep him from building the church.

He called the church that he was going to build the kingdom of heaven. Sometimes when he talked about it he called it the kingdom of God.

There was not a church then. The disciples did not know what Jesus meant when he talked about his church or his kingdom.

He told them many things about it. He said that some of his disciples would not die until the church was built.

He did not build it while he was here on earth. He waited until he went back to heaven.

When he built the church he sent the Holy Spirit to his disciples so they could remember the things he had told them.

The Holy Spirit told them just how to do. He told them what to write when they wrote the New Testament.

QUESTIONS

1. What did Jesus ask his disciples as they were walking along?
2. What did the disciples say?
3. What did Jesus ask them then?
4. What did Peter say?
5. What did Jesus say he was going to build?
6. What did he call the church he was going to build?
7. Did he build the church while he was here on earth?
8. When did he build it?
9. Did he say he would have to be killed be-

fore he built the church?

10. Could anything keep him from doing it?
11. Did the disciples understand all that Jesus told them?
12. Whom did Jesus send after he went to heaven to make them remember and understand what he said?

The Transfiguration
(Luke 9:28-36)

About a week after Jesus had told his disciples that he was going to build his church, he took three of his disciples, Peter, James, and John, and went up into a real high mountain to pray.

While he was praying, the three disciples went to sleep. When they waked up they saw two men talking with Jesus.

Jesus looked different. His face was shining like the sun, and his clothes were white as snow.

The men who were talking with him were Moses and Elijah. They, too, were bright and their clothes were white. They were talking about Jesus' death.

The disciples were afraid. They

did not know what to do or what to say.

Peter said, "Lord, it is good for us to be here. Let us make three tabernacles, one for you, one for Moses, and one for Elijah."

Tabernacles were places to worship. Peter wanted to build a place to worship Jesus, Moses, and Elijah. He really did not know what he was saying because he was so afraid.

A great cloud came up on the mountain. It covered all of them.

The disciples were scared when they entered into the cloud.

A voice came from heaven saying, "This is my beloved Son, in whom I am well pleased. Hear ye him."

The three disciples fell down on their knees.

Jesus came to them and touched them.

When they got up, they saw no one except Jesus.

Jesus told them not to tell anyone what they had seen until after he had risen from the dead.

The disciples began to question each other about what Jesus meant when he said he would rise from the dead. They believed that he was the Son of God. They believed the things he taught them, but they could not understand all the things he told them.

Later when Jesus had died, had gone back to heaven, and had sent the Holy

Spirit to them, they did understand those things, because the Holy Spirit helped them.

QUESTIONS

1. Whom did Jesus take with him up on the high mountain?
2. Why did they go up there?
3. What did the disciples do while Jesus was praying?
4. When they were awake, whom did they see?
5. How did Jesus and Moses and Elijah look?
6. What did Peter say?
7. What came on the mountain and covered them?
8. What did the voice from heaven say?
9. Did Jesus tell the disciples not to tell anybody what they had seen?
10. When did he say they could tell it?
11. Did the disciples understand all he told them?
12. Whom did Jesus send when he went back to heaven to make them remember and understand things?

Jesus Heals a Blind Man

(John 9:1-38)

As Jesus passed by the Temple one day he saw a blind man sitting there begging. The man had been blind all his life.

Jesus spit on the ground, made mud, and put it on the man's eyes.

He said, "Go and wash your eyes in the pool."

The man went and washed his eyes, and he could see.

His neighbors and the people who had seen him begging at the Temple said, "Is this the man that sat here and begged?"

Some said, "Yes, this is he."

Others said, "No, it is not he, but it looks like him."

The man said, "I am he."

They said to him, "How were your eyes opened?"

He answered, "A man named Jesus made mud and put on my eyes. He told me to go wash in the pool, and I went. When I washed my eyes, I could see."

Now, it was the Sabbath day. I have already told you that the Jews could not do any work on that day.

The Sabbath day was Saturday, and the Jews were supposed to rest and study on that day.

The Pharisees were Jews who thought they were good, but Jesus knew they were not. They did not like Jesus because he helped people and healed them on the Sabbath day.

It was not wrong to make people well on the Sabbath day, but they wanted something to say against Jesus.

When the Pharisees saw the man who had been blind, they asked him who made him see. He told them about Jesus and how he had opened his eyes.

They said, "This is a bad man, and he does not do what God wants him to because he works on the Sabbath day."

The man said, "I do not know who he is, but he could not do such wonderful things if he were not a good man and if God were not with him."

That made the Pharisees angry. They did not want anybody to like Jesus.

They called the man's mother and father. They said to them, "Is this your son, and was he born blind?"

The mother and father said, "Yes, this is our son, and he was born blind, but we do not know who made him see. He is old enough to talk, ask him."

They were afraid of the Pharisees, so they would not tell anything about Jesus.

The Pharisees called the man again and asked him how he could see.

The man said, "I have told you already, and you did not believe me. I will not tell you any more."

The Pharisees became very angry. They made the man leave so he could not worship with them any more.

When Jesus heard that they had made the man leave, he found him. He said to him, "Do you believe on the Son of God?

The man said, "Who is he, Lord, that I may believe on him?"

Jesus said, "I am the Son of God."

The man fell down on his knees and worshipped him. He said, "Lord, I believe."

Jesus had made him see just because he wanted him to believe on him. Nobody could do such wonderful things except the Son of God.

QUESTIONS

1. Whom did Jesus see as he passed by the Temple?
2. How long had the man been blind?
3. What did Jesus do?
4. What did he tell the man to do?
5. What did the people say when they saw that the man could see?
6. What did they ask the man?
7. What did he tell them?
8. Why did the Pharisees not like Jesus?
9. When they asked the man who opened his eyes, what did he say?
10. What did they ask his mother and father?
11. What did his mother and father say?
12. When the man would not tell them any more, what did the Pharisees do?
13. When Jesus found the man, what did he say?
14. What did the man say?

The Good Shepherd

(John 10:1-18)

Jesus often told the people stories as he talked to them to make them understand what he meant. One day he told them this story that we call "The Good Shepherd."

In that country many of the people had sheep.

When the weather was pretty and warm the sheep stayed out in the fields where they could get plenty of green grass to eat.

When the weather was cold, they stayed inside in a place called the "fold," or the "sheep fold."

There was always a man who took care of the sheep. He was the shepherd. When he started to take his sheep out of the fold into the field he would go to the door and call the sheep.

The man who kept the door shut would open the door and let him in. The sheep knew his voice and would follow him out.

The shepherd would call all his sheep by their names and lead them out. He did not drive them, but they knew him and would follow him.

Sometimes some wicked people would come and try to steal the sheep. They would not go to the door and call the sheep because the sheep would not know their voice and would not follow them. The robbers would sometimes climb up over the walls and try to get the sheep.

Sometimes a shepherd would pay a man to look after his sheep.

When a wolf would come out of the woods and try to kill some of the sheep, the man would be afraid and run away. He would not love the sheep and take care of them because they were not his.

Jesus said, "I am the good shepherd. I know my sheep, and they know me."

He called those people who loved him his "sheep." He looked after them just as a good shepherd looks after his sheep.

Other men came trying to teach the people things that were wrong just as robbers came to steal the sheep, but

Jesus taught them the things that were right.

Jesus said he would give his life for his sheep.

That meant he would die before he would let anything happen to the people that believed on him. He loves everybody and always takes care of us.

He wants us to listen to everything he says and follow him. We are following him when we do what he tells us to do.

We can not really hear Jesus talking

now as those people did then, but the things he did are written in the Bible.

When we read the Bible we are listening to Jesus talk.

QUESTIONS

1. What did Jesus often tell the people?
2. What is the name of this story?
3. Where did the sheep stay in pretty weather?
4. Where did they stay in bad weather?
5. What was the man called who took care of the sheep?
6. Did he know the sheep and call them by their names?
7. Would they follow him?
8. How did the robbers try to get the sheep?
9. Who did Jesus say he was?
10. Who are Jesus' sheep?
11. Did Jesus say he loved his sheep so much he would die before he would let anything happen to them?
12. Can we really hear Jesus talking now?
13. How do we know what he wants us to do?

The Story of the Good Samaritan

(Luke 10:25-37)

One day a lawyer came to Jesus and asked him what he must do to get to go to heaven and live with God when he died.

Jesus asked him what was written in the Bible.

He said, "Thou shalt love the Lord thy God with all thy heart, and with all thy soul and with all thy strength, and with all thy mind, and thy neighbor as thyself."

Jesus answered, "You have answered right. If you do these things you will live."

The lawyer did not want to love his neighbor as he should so he said, "Who is my neighbor?"

Jesus told him this story:

A man was going down from Jerusalem to Jericho, and he fell among robbers.

That means that some very wicked people came and took everything he had away from him. They even took his good clothes off him and left him half-naked.

They beat him until he was nearly dead. When they had taken everything he had and left him nearly dead, they went away leaving him lying by the side of the road. They did not care if he died.

A priest came along the road and saw the poor man.

I have told you that a priest was a man who worked in the Temple and talked to God for the people. He should have been a real good man and one who would help anybody who was sick or in trouble. This priest saw the man lying beside the road all beaten, nearly naked, and nearly dead, but he did not stay to help him. He just went by on the other side and acted as if he had not seen him.

After a while a Levite came by and saw the man lying by the side of the road.

A Levite was a man who helped the priests around the Temple. He should have known what God wanted him to do because he stayed around the Temple so much where the people worshipped.

When the Levite saw the poor man lying there nearly dead he acted just as the priest did. He passed by on the other side of the road.

Finally a Samaritan came by.

A Samaritan was a man that the priest and the Levite would not even talk to. They thought they were better than the Samaritans.

The Samaritan saw the man lying by the side of the road. He was very sorry for him.

He went to him, wrapped up the sores that the wicked men had made when they beat him, and put medicine on them.

He picked the man up, put him on his donkey that he was riding, and carried him to an inn. An inn was a place where people who were traveling could spend the night.

The Samaritan took care of the poor man all night.

The next day when he had to leave, he gave the innkeeper some money. He told him to take care of the man until he was well and strong again.

He said, "If this is not enough money, when I come back I will give you some more."

Jesus then told the lawyer that he must do good to everybody who needed him.

QUESTIONS

1. What did the lawyer ask Jesus?
2. What question did Jesus ask him?
3. Can you learn the verse that the lawyer told Jesus?
4. Did the lawyer want to love his neighbor as he should?
5. What did he ask about his neighbor?
6. In the story that Jesus told, what happened to the man who was traveling?
7. Who came by and saw the poor man?
8. What did the priest do?
9. After a while who else came by?
10. What did the Levite do?
11. Who was the third man who came along?
12. What did the good Samaritan do?
13. When the Samaritan took the sick man to the inn, why did he give the innkeeper some money?
14. What did he say he would do if the innkeeper needed more money?
15. Must we do good to everybody who needs help?

Jesus Teaches His Disciples To Pray

(Matt. 6:5-13)

As Jesus was praying one day, his disciples came to him. They said, "Lord, teach us to pray as John taught his disciples."

Jesus began then to tell them how they should pray so that God would hear them.

He told them not to pray as some people did out on the streets just so others could see them. Some of these people would stand in the street and talk real loud so everybody who was passing by could hear them. They would use lots of words and say the same things again and again to make others think they were real good. Jesus said that God would not hear a prayer like that.

He told his disciples to go into a room alone and talk to God where nobody else could hear. God can see and hear when people cannot. He could hear a prayer that the disciples prayed when nobody else was there.

Jesus told his disciples to pray like this:

"Our Father, who art in heaven,
Hallowed be thy name.
Thy kingdom come.
Thy will be done in earth as it is in heaven.

Give us this day our daily bread. And forgive us our debts as we forgive our debtors.

And lead us not into temptation, but deliver us from evil.

For thine is the kingdom, and the power, and the glory forever.

Amen."

This prayer is usually called "The Lord's Prayer," but it is really the prayer that Jesus taught his disciples to pray. He did not mean for all people everywhere to pray it.

We can pray for some of the things he taught them to pray for.

We can pray for God to give us our food every day.

We can pray for him to forgive us of the things we do that are wrong.

We can pray that God's will may be done on earth as it is in heaven.

We must pray for those things, but we cannot pray "Thy kingdom come." Jesus taught his disciples to pray that because they were looking for the kingdom, and he had told them that it would come.

We cannot pray now for the kingdom to come because it has already come. The church is the kingdom, and Jesus built the church soon after he left the earth and went back to heaven.

We must be very careful not to ask for things in our prayers that are selfish. We must pray for things that will help other people as well as ourselves.

God wants us to talk to him and ask him for the things we need. He wants us to know that he gives us everything, so he has told us to pray again and again to him.

Boys and girls should learn to pray to God real often. We could not even live if God did not give us air to breathe, food to eat, and other things we need.

QUESTIONS

1. When Jesus was praying, what did his disciples tell him to do?
2. How did some people pray?

3. Did Jesus want his disciples to pray on the streets so people could see them?
4. Where did he tell them to go to pray?
5. Did Jesus tell them how they should pray?
6. What is this prayer usually called?
7. What should we call it?
8. Did he mean for people everywhere to pray this prayer?
9. Name some of the things in this prayer that we can pray for.
10. What is in the prayer that we cannot pray?
11. Why did Jesus tell his disciples to pray "Thy kingdom come"?
12. Why can we not pray for that?
13. What is the kingdom?
14. Who built the church?
15. When did the kingdom or church come?
16. Will God hear our prayers if we are selfish and do not think about others?
17. Does God know what we need?
18. Why does he want us to pray?

The Foolish Rich Man

(Luke 12:13-21)

As Jesus was teaching the people a great multitude was listening. There came a man out of the crowd and said to him, "Lord, tell my brother to give me part of the money that our father gave us."

Jesus told him that he did not come to divide things for them. He had something else to do.

He told the crowd then to be careful not to think too much about money.

He said that there are other things more important than the money a person has or the other things he may get.

He told them this story:

There was once a very rich man who had lots of grain on his farm.

So much grew that he had no place to store it. His barns were running over.

He said, "What shall I do? I do not have room to store my grain."

He said, "I know what I will do. I will tear down my barns and build bigger ones, and I will put my grain in the big barns. When I have all this good grain put up, I will just eat, drink, and be happy because I have so much laid up that I will not have to worry for a long time."

God heard what the rich man said. He said to him, "Thou foolish one. To-night you shall die, and then whose shall all these things be that you have laid up?"

Jesus said that would be the way of everybody who tried to get a lot of money in this life and did not think about God.

He taught his disciples to help the poor and do good to every one instead of saving all they could get.

God does not like a selfish person. He will not let a selfish person go to heaven.

The rich man in the story should have given away all the grain that he could not use. Then God would have been pleased with him.

One time Jesus told his disciples that it is easier for a camel to go through the eye of a needle than for a rich man to go to heaven. A person can not love money and love God, too.

We must use our money to do the things God has told us to do.

QUESTIONS

1. When Jesus was teaching the people what did a man ask him?
2. Did Jesus come to divide money for people?
3. What kind of a man did Jesus tell them about in his story?
4. What did the rich man say he would do to have room for his grain?
5. What was he going to do when he got his grain all laid up?
6. Did he think about God or poor people?
7. What did God say to him?
8. What did Jesus teach his disciples to do with their money?
9. Does God like a selfish person?

10. What should the rich man have done with the grain he did not need?
11. How hard did Jesus say it would be for a rich man to go to heaven?
12. Can a person love money and love God too?

The Lost Sheep and the Lost Money

(Luke 15:3-10)

Jesus told the people a story about a man who had a hundred sheep.

One day when he was taking them in from the pasture to the fold where they were to spend the night, he saw that one sheep was gone.

He had ninety-nine there, but he left them and went out to look for the **one** that was lost. He looked and **looked** until he found it.

Then he took it up in his arms, put it on his shoulder, and carried it home to be with the others.

When he got there he called all his friends to him and said, "Be happy with me because I have found my sheep that was lost."

Jesus told them another story about something that was lost.

A woman had ten pieces of money, and she lost one.

She took the broom, swept the house, and looked real closely until she found the piece that was lost.

When she found it she called in her friends and said to them, "Be happy with me because I have found the piece of money that I had lost."

Jesus said that he came down from heaven to save people who were lost. People are lost when they do not love God and do not obey him.

Jesus helps us do what is right. He said that the angels in heaven are happy when one person stops doing wrong and does what is right. They are just like the man who found his lost sheep and the woman who found her lost money.

QUESTIONS

1. How many sheep did the man have in the story that Jesus told?
2. What happened to one of them?
3. What did the man do?
4. How did he take the sheep home when he found it?
5. Did he call his friends to come?
6. What did he tell them?
7. What did the woman in the other story have?
8. What happened to one piece of her money?
9. What did she do?
10. Did she call her friends?
11. What did she tell them to do?

12. What did Jesus say he came down from heaven to do?
13. Are people lost when they do not love God and obey him?
14. How do the angels feel when one person stops doing bad things and does right?

The Lost Boy

(Luke 15:11-32)

In our last story Jesus told about the lost sheep and the lost money.

He told another story about something else that was lost.

The other thing that was lost was worth more than a sheep or a piece of money. It was a man's son.

A man had two sons.

One of them was not happy at home and wanted to go away. One day he said to his father, "Give me the part of your money that belongs to me."

When a man dies he leaves his money to his children. This boy wanted his part while his father was still living.

The father divided all his money between the two boys.

Not many days after that the younger boy, who was not happy at home, left and went to a country a long way off. He did not even want to see his father or brother. He took all his money with him, so he thought he could have a good time.

The boy found lots of friends because he had plenty of money to buy them nice things. He lived just as he wanted to because his father was not there to tell him not to do anything. He did some very bad things. He just wasted his money until after a while he did not have any left. He did not have any friends then because they were wicked and did not like him when he did not have any more money to spend. He did not have any food, and he was hungry.

He went to work for a man, but the man did not give him food to eat or clothes to wear. He had to feed the hogs. He was so hungry he thought he could eat the food he was giving the hogs.

One day he began to think of his old home and his father.

He said, "The servants that work at my father's house have more food than they can eat, and I am about to starve. I am going back to my father, and I am going to say, 'Father, I have done wrong to God and to you, and I am too bad to be your son any more. Let me be one of your servants'."

He got up and started home.

Before he got there his father saw him and ran to meet him. He hugged and kissed him.

The boy started to tell him that he had done wrong and was too bad to be called his son any more, but his father would not let him say it.

He said to one of his servants, "Bring some good clothes and put on him. Put a ring on his finger. Put shoes on his feet. Kill the fat calf, and let us be happy. My son was lost and now is found."

They killed the fat calf and cooked it. They fixed lots of good things to eat, and they were laughing and singing because they were so happy.

The older boy was out in the field. He heard them singing and playing. He called a servant and asked why they were happy. The servant told him that his brother had come home again.

The older boy was angry and would not go into the house.

His father came out and begged him to come in.

The boy said, "I stayed at home and did not go away and waste money. I did not live a wicked life, and you never did kill a fat calf for me and let me have a good time with my friends, but when this wicked boy comes back you are happy."

The father said, "We ought to be happy because this boy was lost and now he is found again. He was dead and is alive again."

He meant that the boy had come home to those who loved him and wanted to do right again.

QUESTIONS

1. What was lost in this story that Jesus told?
2. How many sons did the man have?
3. Were they both happy at home?

4. What did the younger son ask his father to give him?
5. Did the father give him some money?
6. What did the boy do after that?
7. When he left home did he do good things or bad things?
8. Did he waste his money until it was all gone?
9. Did he get hungry?
10. What did he say he would do?
11. Did he think he was good enough to be called a son any more?
12. When he got nearly home who came running to meet him?
13. What did he do when he met him?
14. What did the father tell his servant?
15. Was the older brother angry when he heard them laughing and singing?
16. Why did the father say they should be happy?

The Rich Man and Lazarus

(Luke 16:19-31)

When Jesus was teaching the people, he often told stories. We have heard some of his stories.

One day he told them about a wicked rich man and a good poor man.

The rich man wore fine clothes every day and had lots of good things to eat. He did not care about anybody but himself.

There was a poor man who had only ragged clothes to wear and had nothing to eat.

Every day some one brought him and laid him at the gate of the rich man's yard.

The poor man's name was Lazarus. He was sick and hungry. He had sores

all over his body, and nobody came to take care of him. The dogs often came and licked his sores. He lay at the rich man's gate hoping to get some food, maybe the crumbs that were left after the rich man had eaten.

After a time the poor sick man died. Angels carried him away up to heaven with God, where Abraham lived.

He had been a good man, so he could live with God and with all the other good people who had died.

The rich man died too, but angels did not take him to heaven. He had been a wicked man, so he had to go to the place where bad people are punished for their sins.

He was punished so much that he was very, very sorry for the way he had lived.

He looked up and saw Lazarus in heaven. He cried to Abraham to send him down to help him.

Abraham said, "Do you not remember that while you were alive you had lots of good things and Lazarus had bad things? Now he is happy, and you are sad."

He told the rich man that no one could leave heaven and go down to where the wicked people were. No one could leave the wicked place to go to heaven.

The rich man was sadder than ever and begged Abraham to let Lazarus rise from the dead, go back to the world, and tell his five brothers to be good and not go where he was.

Abraham would not send Lazarus back to the world.

He said the people in the world have the Bible to teach them how to live right. If they do not do what it says they would not listen if some one came back from the dead.

QUESTIONS

1. Who were the two men that Jesus told about in this story?
2. How did the poor man dress?
3. How did the rich man dress?
4. Which one was good?
5. Where did the poor man lie every day?
6. What did he want?
7. When the poor man died who came and carried him up to live with God?

8. Did the angels take the rich man to heaven?

9. Why did the rich man have to be punished?

10. Did the rich man want Lazarus to come down and help him?

11. Would God send the poor man down to him?

12. What else did the rich man want Lazarus to do?

13. Why would God not send Lazarus back to the earth?

14. Why did Jesus come to the world?

The Story of Lazarus
(John 11:1-46)

Mary, Martha, and Lazarus lived in a little town called Bethany.

Mary and Martha were sisters, and Lazarus was their brother.

Jesus loved them and often went to see them. He spent many nights in their home and told them about God.

They loved Jesus and believed that he was the Son of God.

One day Mary and Martha sent to Jesus to tell him that Lazarus was sick. They said, "The one you love is sick."

Jesus did not go to see him then, but waited a while where he was. After a few days he told his disciples that he was going to see Lazarus.

The disciples begged him not to go

because the Jews were trying to kill him. But he said that he must go. Then he told them that Lazarus was dead.

They started to go to Bethany where Mary, Martha, and Lazarus lived.

Before they got there Martha heard that they were coming and ran to meet them. When she got to them, she fell down on the ground by Jesus and cried.

She said, "Lord, if you had been here my brother would not have died."

Jesus said to her, "Your brother will rise again." She said, "I know he will rise again at the last day."

Jesus told her to believe on him and her brother would live again. She said, "I believe that you are the Son of God."

Martha ran back to the house and told Mary that Jesus had come.

Mary went out of the house and ran to meet him. When she met him, she

fell down on the ground and said, "Lord, if you had been here my brother would not have died."

When Jesus saw her crying and all her friends with her crying, he was sad. Jesus cried too.

The people said, "Look how much he loved him."

Jesus said, "Where have you buried him?"

They took him to the place.

They had not dug a grave as people do now. They had buried him in a cave and rolled a big stone over the door.

Jesus said, "Take away the stone."

Martha said, "Lord, he has been dead four days now, and his body will smell bad."

They took away the stone though because Jesus said do it. Jesus looked up into the sky and prayed to God. He

cried with a loud voice, "Lazarus, come forth."

Lazarus came out of the grave with his hands and feet all wrapped in grave clothes and his face wrapped in a cloth.

Jesus said, "Take the grave clothes off and let him go."

Many of the people who were with Mary and Martha believed that Jesus was the Son of God.

Some of the people were angry at him though because he could do so many wonderful things, and they did not want to believe him. They began to try to think of some way to kill him.

QUESTIONS

1. Name the two sisters and their brother who lived in Bethany.
2. Did Jesus love them?
3. What bad thing happened to Lazarus?
4. When Jesus was coming to Bethany who ran out to meet him?
5. What did she tell him?
6. Did he tell her that Lazarus would live again?
7. When Jesus saw Mary and the others crying, what did he do?
8. Did he ask where they had buried Lazarus?
9. When they got to the grave what did he tell them to do?
10. Why did they not want to take away the stone?
11. How long had Lazarus been dead?
12. When they took the stone away what did Jesus do?

13. What did Lazarus do?
14. Did Mary, Martha, and many of the others believe that he was the Son of God?
15. Did all of them believe in him?

Ten Men Made Well

(Luke 17:11-19)

One day Jesus and his disciples were going up to Jerusalem.

As they passed through one of the little towns, ten men came to meet them. They were sick men. They had a very bad disease called leprosy.

Doctors could not cure leprosy, so the people who had it had to leave their homes and live away from other people. That was to keep others from taking it.

When the ten men came out of the city to meet Jesus, they did not come up close to him. They stood a long way off.

They cried out to him in a loud voice and said, "Jesus, Master, have mercy on us." They wanted him to do something for them.

When Jesus saw them he called to them and said, "Go and show yourselves to the priests."

They minded Jesus and turned to go. As they went they discovered that they were well.

One of them, when he saw that he was well, ran back to Jesus, fell down before him, and thanked him for making him well.

Jesus said unto him, "Were there not ten men healed? Where are the nine?" Only one man out of the ten who were made well came back to say "Thank you" to Jesus.

Jesus was pleased with him, but he was sorry about the others who forgot to say "Thank you."

He told the man to get up and go home. He said, "your faith has made you well." That meant that he was healed because he believed in Jesus.

I hope that we do not do as the nine men did. We must always remember to thank God for all he has done for us.

We must thank him every day for the things he gives us every day: our lives, our homes, those we love, and everything we have.

We should thank people, too, for

doing things for us. Jesus is pleased when we say "Thank you."

QUESTIONS

1. Who came to meet Jesus out of one of the little towns?
2. What was the matter with the men?
3. What did they want Jesus to do for them?
4. What did Jesus tell them to do?
5. When they started to go, what did they discover?
6. What did one man do?
7. What did Jesus say to him?
8. Was Jesus pleased because he remembered to say "Thank you"?
9. Was he sorry that the others did not come back to say "Thank you"?
10. Should we always remember to tell God "Thank You" for all the things he has done for us?

The Young Rich Man

(Luke 18:18-27)

A young man came to Jesus one day and said, "Good Master, what must I do so that I may go heaven when I die?"

Jesus said to him, "Why do you call me good? There is no one good except God."

The young man was very rich, but he must have been a good man because when Jesus looked at him he loved him.

He said, "If you want to go to heaven you must do the things God has said. You must not take things that belong to other people. You must not kill. You must not tell things that are not true about people. You must obey your parents, and you must love your neighbors."

172

The young rich man said, "I have kept all these things ever since I was a boy. What else must I do?"

Jesus said, "If you want to do all that God wants you to do, go sell everything you have and give it to poor people. Then come and follow me."

The young man was very sad when he heard that. He had lots of money and lots of other things. He did not want to give away what he had. He went away very sad and did not do what Jesus said.

When he was gone Jesus said to his disciples, "It is hard for a rich man to go to heaven." Then he said, "It is easier for a camel to go through the eye of a needle than for a rich man to go to heaven."

The disciples were surprised. They said, "Who then can be saved?"

Jesus told them that God would know that, and he can do things that men can not do. He told them one time that some people would do all kinds of wicked things for money.

We must not want money just to keep or to use just for ourselves. We must use all we get to help others. We are giving our money to Jesus when we help others with it.

QUESTIONS

1. What did the young man ask Jesus?
2. What did Jesus tell the young man he must do to get to go to heaven?
3. Did the young man have a great deal of money?
4. What did Jesus tell him to do with his money?
5. Did the young man want to give his money to poor people?
6. Was he very sad because Jesus told him that?
7. Is it hard for a rich man to go to heaven?
8. How should we always use our money?

The Story of a Short Man
(Luke 19:1-10)

Jesus went into a city called Jericho and passed through on his way to Jerusalem.

There was a man named Zacchaeus who lived in Jericho. He was a rich man.

The Jews did not like him because he was one who collected taxes for the government. That meant he gathered up money from the people for the rulers. The people did not like to give the money.

The men who took up the money often took up too much, and they often kept part of it for themselves. Zacchaeus had been keeping too much for himself.

When Jesus passed through Jericho, Zacchaeus wanted to see him.

He ran down the road where he knew Jesus would come.

He was a real short man and could not see over the crowd.

He ran ahead of all the people and climbed up into a tree so he could see Jesus when he passed under the tree.

When Jesus came under the tree he stopped and looked up into the tree.

He said, "Zacchaeus, come down quickly because I am going home with you."

Zacchaeus came down quickly. He carried Jesus home with him. He was very happy.

When the people saw that Jesus had gone home with him, they said he should not have gone. They said that Zacchaeus was a sinner. That meant he had done wrong things. Jesus went to his house to teach him to do right.

While Jesus was visiting in his house, Zacchaeus stood up and said, "I am going to give half of everything I have to the poor people. If I have taken money from people that I should not, I will give them four times as much as I took."

Jesus said to him, "Today has salvation come to your house." That meant that he had learned that day what was right, and he was going to do what Jesus wanted him to do.

Jesus said he came down from heaven to find people who were doing wrong and to teach them how to do the right things so they may live with God when they die.

QUESTIONS

1. What was the name of the man in our story who lived at Jericho?
2. Did the Jews like him?

3. Did Zacchaeus want to see Jesus?
4. Why did he not go into the crowd to see him?
5. Where did he get so he could see him?
6. When Jesus got under the tree, what did he tell Zacchaeus to do?
7. Did the people say Jesus had done wrong when he went into Zacchaeus' house?
8. What did Zacchaeus say he would do if he had taken too much money from people?
9. Was Jesus glad when Zacchaeus wanted to do right?
10. Why did Jesus say he came down from heaven?

Jesus Rides into Jerusalem
(Luke 19:28-41)

Jesus and his disciples were walking up toward the city of Jerusalem. They passed through the little town of Bethany where Lazarus lived whom Jesus raised from the dead.

Before they came to Bethany Jesus sent two of his disciples ahead into the town.

He told them to go into the little town and there they would find a colt tied. He told them to untie him and bring him.

He said if the man who owned the colt asked them why they were untying him, they were to say, "The Lord needs him."

The two disciples went just as Jesus

told them, and when they entered into the town they found the colt standing tied. They remembered what Jesus told them to do and started to untie him.

As they were untying him, the man who owned him said, "Why are you untying the colt?"

They answered, "The Lord needs him."

The man who owned him let them take him, so they brought him to Jesus.

No one had ever ridden on this colt. When they brought him to Jesus they put their coats on him, and Jesus got on him to ride.

Some of the other people laid their coats on the ground for Jesus to ride on. He started riding into the city of Jerusalem.

When the people in the city heard that Jesus was coming, they came running out to meet him.

Some of them put their coats on the ground. Others cut branches of the trees and spread them down on the ground. They made a carpet for Jesus to ride on. That was the way they did when a king rode into a city.

They thought he was going into Jerusalem to be their king.

They sang and shouted praises to him. They said, "Hosanna. Blessed is he that comes in the name of the Lord."

A great crowd ran along with him shouting and singing as they ran.

Some of the Pharisees, the leaders of the people who thought they were good when they were really wicked, were very angry when they saw the crowd. They did not like Jesus, and they did not like to see other people following him.

When Jesus got in sight of Jerusalem, he looked over all the city and cried because the people in it were wicked and would not obey him.

He wanted them to do right, but they would not listen to him.

He said, "I would like to gather you together as a hen gathers her chickens under her wings, but you will not let me."

QUESTIONS

1. Why did Jesus send two of his disciples into the town?
2. Did the disciples find the colt just as Jesus said?
3. When they were untying the colt what did the man say who owned the colt?
4. What did the disciples say?
5. Had any one ever ridden on this colt?
6. What did the people put on the colt for Jesus to sit on?
7. What did they spread down on the ground?
8. Was this the way people treated a king when he rode into a city?
9. Did the people shout and cry to Jesus?
10. Did the Pharisees like for the people to be following Jesus?
11. What did Jesus do when he got in sight of the city?
12. Why did he cry?

Cleansing the Temple

(Matt. 21:12-17)

After Jesus had ridden into the city of Jerusalem on the colt, he went into the Temple where the people gathered to worship God.

When he got there he saw a crowd of men who were buying and selling things right in the Temple. They had cows and sheep in there.

They sold these animals to the people who came to worship God. God wanted them to kill the animals and burn them on an altar. We call it offering sacrifice to God.

These wicked people had brought the animals into the Temple, and they sold them for too much money.

Jesus drove all the animals out of the Temple.

He made the wicked men leave, too.

He turned over the tables on which they kept their money.

It made him angry to see the way the wicked people were using the Temple.

He said, "My house is a house of prayer, and you have made it a den of robbers."

This made the leaders of the people very angry for Jesus to drive out the animals and those who sold them.

They said, "What right does he have to do this?"

They began to wonder how they could kill him. They were afraid to do anything to him because lots of the people loved him and followed him wherever he went.

Jesus did not stop doing good things because the leaders wanted to kill him. That very day while they were angry with him he made many sick people well.

That made them more angry, but the people who were made well were happy.

When night came Jesus and his disciples left Jerusalem. They went out to the little town of Bethany to spend the night.

They probably stayed with Mary, Martha, and Lazarus. Jesus loved them, and they loved him, so he liked to visit them.

QUESTIONS

1. Where did Jesus go when he got to the city?
2. What did he find in the Temple?
3. Was he angry when he saw the animals in the Temple?
4. What did Jesus do to the animals and to the men who were selling them?
5. Did it make the people very angry when he drove them out?
6. Did they begin to wonder how they could kill him?
7. Did Jesus stop doing good things just because the people became angry?
8. What did he do to the sick people that very day?
9. Did it make the leaders of the people more angry than ever when he made sick people well?
10. Where did Jesus go to spend the night?

Five Wise Girls and Five Foolish Girls

(Matt. 25:1-13)

Jesus told his disciples a story about ten girls. They are called virgins.

A virgin is a girl that is not married.

A man had been married, and he was giving a great feast as people did in those days.

The ten virgins were going to the feast. They got ready to meet the bridegroom, or the man who had been married. They did not know what time he would come.

It was night, so they took their lamps with them.

Five of the girls took more oil for their lamps so they would have plenty if the bridegroom was a long time coming.

Five of the girls did not take any extra oil. They thought they had enough oil in their lamps to last.

The girls who carried extra oil for their lamps are called wise virgins. Those who did not carry extra oil are called foolish virgins.

The bridegroom did not come for a long time. While they waited all the girls went to sleep.

After a while some one called, "The bridegroom is coming."

All the girls got up quickly and started to meet him.

The five foolish girls said to the wise girls, "Give us some of your oil because our lamps are going out."

The wise girls answered, "We can not because there is not enough for us and you, too. You go to the man who sells oil and buy some."

The foolish girls went to buy some oil. While they were gone, the bridegroom came. The wise girls were ready, so they went with him to the feast.

When the foolish girls came back they saw the door shut.

They knocked at the door and begged the bridegroom to let them in. He would not let them in because they were late. They should have been ready when he came.

Jesus said that when he comes back from heaven he will come as the bridegroom did. No one will know just when he will come.

We must do all we can to be ready when he comes so he will let us go with him to heaven.

QUESTIONS

1. How many girls were there in the story Jesus told?
2. Where were they going?

3. Did they know what time the bridegroom would come?
4. What did they take with them?
5. Did all the girls take some extra oil along?
6. What did they all do while they waited?
7. When the bridegroom came what did the foolish girls ask the wise girls to give them?
8. Why would the wise girls not give the foolish girls some of their oil?
9. Where did the foolish girls have to go?
10. When they got back could they get into the house?
11. Why could they not get into the house?
12. Does any one know when Jesus is coming back from heaven?
13. Did he tell us to do all we can to be ready when he comes?
14. Will he take us to heaven with him if we are doing right when he comes?

The Sheep and the Goats
(Matt. 25:31-46)

Jesus told his disciples another story about when he will come back from heaven at the last day.

He said that he would come back and bring all the angels with him.

Then all the people of the world will see him, and he will separate the good from the bad just as a shepherd separates the sheep from the goats.

Jesus called the good people the sheep, and he will put them on his right side.

He called the bad people the goats, and he will put them on his left side.

He will say to the good people on his right side, "Come into heaven and enjoy the good things that my Father has

made for you. For I was hungry, and
you gave me food to eat. I was thirsty,
and you gave me water to drink. I was
naked, and you gave me clothes to
wear. I was sick, and you visited me.
I was in prison, and you came to me."

The good people will say, "When did we see you hungry and give you food? When did we see you thirsty and give you water? When did we see you sick or in prison and come to see you?"

Then Jesus will say, "When you have done any of these things to the people in the world you have done them to me."

He will say to the wicked people on his left side, "Go away to be punished with the devil and his angels. I was hungry, and you gave me no food. I was thirsty, and you gave me no drink. I was a stranger, and you took me not in. I was naked, and you gave me no clothes. I was sick and in prison, and you did not visit me."

Then the wicked people will answer and say, "Lord, when did we see you hungry, or thirsty, or a stranger, or naked, or sick, or in prison, and did not give you the things you needed?"

Jesus said to them, "When you found some of the people in the world who needed these things and you did not help them, you did not help me."

The wicked then will have to go away from Jesus into the place to be punished where the devil and his angels have to stay.

The good people will get to go to heaven where they can live forever with God, Jesus, and the good angels.

QUESTIONS

1. When Jesus comes back from heaven, whom will he bring with him?
2. How will Jesus separate the people of the world?
3. What does Jesus call the good people?
4. What does Jesus call the bad people?
5. What will he say to the good people?
6. What will they say to him?
7. When do we do good things to Jesus?

8. What will he say to the bad people?
9. What will they say to him?
10. When do we do bad things to Jesus?
11. Where will the wicked people have to go?
12. Where will the good people get to go?

Mary Shows Her Love for Jesus
(John 12:1-9)

Now when Jesus was at Bethany he went into the house of a man named Simon.

Mary, Martha, and Lazarus were there, too.

They made a supper for Jesus and others whom they had invited.

Martha helped to prepare the food and serve it. She was always interested in serving food to her guests and making them comfortable. She became angry with Mary one time because she would not help her.

Mary liked to sit and listen to Jesus talk. Jesus said that was more important than preparing food to eat.

At the supper where Martha was

serving, Lazarus sat at the table to eat with Jesus. You remember that Jesus had raised him from the dead after he had been in the grave for four days.

While they were sitting at the table, Mary came to Jesus bringing a box of very precious ointment or perfume. That means she had paid a great deal of money for it.

She opened the box and poured the ointment on Jesus' feet. She wiped his feet with her hair.

The ointment smelled very sweet, and soon the whole room was filled with the odor until it smelled sweet, too.

Mary loved Jesus and put the ointment on his feet to show him how much she loved him.

Now Jesus' disciples were with him, and they saw what Mary did. One of them, named Judas, said, "Why did she waste this precious ointment? Why did she not sell it and give the money to the poor?"

He was wicked and did not care about the poor people, but he wanted the money. He was wishing he could have the money for the ointment.

Jesus did not like what Judas said. He was glad that Mary had shown him that she loved him.

He said, "Let her alone. She has done a good thing. You always have poor people with you, but you will not always have me."

Then he said, "Everywhere people tell the story of the gospel, they will tell what Mary has done."

He wanted people everywhere to know that she had been kind and good to him. That is why I am telling you about it now.

There was a crowd of people who came in to the supper, not to eat, and not to see Jesus. They came to see Lazarus. They wanted to see a man who had been dead four days and who was alive again.

Some other people came, too. They came to try to find something bad about Jesus. They wanted to kill him.

They tried to kill Lazarus, too, because the crowd who came to see him believed that Jesus was the Son of God. They knew he could make a dead man come to life again.

QUESTIONS

1. Into whose house did Jesus go to eat supper?
2. Name some other people who were there?
3. Who helped to serve the food?
4. What had Jesus done to Lazarus one time?

5. What did Mary bring to Jesus?
6. What did she do with the ointment?
7. With what did she wipe Jesus' feet?
8. What did Judas say should have been done with the ointment?
9. Did he love poor people?
10. Did he want the money for the ointment to keep for himself?
11. What did Jesus say about Mary?
12. Did he want people everywhere to know what she did?
13. Why did some of the people come to the supper?
14. Why did the wicked people want to kill Lazarus?

Judas Plans To Do Wrong

(Matt. 26:14-16)

Soon after Jesus was baptized and began to teach the people, you remember that he called twelve men to him and kept them with him wherever he went. These men were called apostles.

Jesus taught them many things that he did not teach the multitude of people who followed him. He was training them for a special work.

He wanted them to be ready to teach people after he went back to heaven.

The names of the twelve apostles were: Peter, Andrew, James, John, Philip, Bartholomew, Thomas, Matthew, James the son of Alphaeus, Simon, Thaddaeus, and Judas.

Eleven of these apostles loved Jesus very much and wanted to learn what he was teaching.

One of them, Judas, did not love Jesus. He was a wicked man.

When the other apostles and Jesus had some money to use for food or to give to poor people, Judas did not like it. He was the one who scolded Mary when she poured out the precious perfume on Jesus' feet because he wanted the money for it.

One day Judas went to the chief priests and the rulers who hated Jesus. He asked them what they would give him if he would bring Jesus to them.

They wanted to kill Jesus. They would be glad for Judas to bring him to them or tell them where they could find him. They told him they would give him thirty pieces of money if he would help them get Jesus.

Judas loved money, so he was glad. He took the thirty pieces of money and left them.

He began to try to think of some way that he could find Jesus alone. He was afraid to do anything when there was a crowd of people around. The people liked to listen to Jesus talk.

Jesus knew that Judas was wicked and that he was trying to help the wicked rulers kill him. But Jesus had a special work to do while he was here, and no one could stop him until he had finished it. Judas could not do anything until Jesus let him.

QUESTIONS

1. How many men did Jesus call to be with him?
2. What were these men called?

3. Can you name the apostles?

4. How many of them loved Jesus?

5. Which one was wicked and did not love Jesus?

6. What did Judas ask the wicked rulers and chief priests?

7. How many pieces of money did they say they would give him?

8. Did Judas want the money?

9. Why was Judas afraid to do anything to Jesus when a crowd was around?

10. Did Jesus know that Judas was wicked?

11. Could any one hurt Jesus until he had finished his work?

The Feast of the Passover

(Mk. 14:12-21, John 13:1-17)

The Jews had a feast every year that was called the Passover.

They kept this feast to remember the time when their fathers and grandfathers were slaves down in the land of Egypt.

They were treated very badly and were unhappy. God sent a man to Egypt to tell his people to leave, but the wicked king would not let them leave the land. He wanted them to work for him.

God punished him in many ways. He refused to let the people go until God sent an angel who passed over the land one night and killed the oldest child in every home of the people of Egypt. He did not kill any of the children in the homes of God's people.

God told the people to keep a feast every year to remember that their children were saved when the angel passed over the land.

While Jesus was here on earth he kept the Passover feast just as the other Jews did. We do not keep it now because he did not tell us to.

When the day came for them to get ready for the Passover, Jesus' disciples came to him and asked him, "Where do you want us to prepare the Passover?"

He called Peter and John to him. He sent them into the town. He told them that as they entered the town they would see a man carrying a pitcher of water. They were to follow him and when he went into a house, they were to ask the owner of the house to show

them the guest room. They must get things ready for the feast.

The two disciples did just as Jesus told them to do. They found the man carrying the pitcher of water, and they

followed him into the house. They found the guest room, and they made everything ready for the feast.

When it was evening Jesus and his twelve disciples came to the house and sat down to eat.

Jesus told them that this would be the last supper he would eat with them before he was put to death.

During the supper Jesus got up from the table. He took a towel and a basin of water, and began to wash the disciples' feet.

When he came to Peter he started to wash his feet too, but Peter said, "You shall never wash my feet."

Jesus told him he could have no part with him in his work if he did not wash his feet.

Peter said, "Not only my feet, but also my hands and my head." He wanted to please Jesus.

When Jesus had finished he sat down again to the table. He began to tell his disciples why he had washed their feet.

They had been disputing among themselves over who was the greatest.

Jesus was greater than any of them, but he had shown them that to be great they must do things for one another.

They must be willing to do anything for others that needed to be done and not feel that they were better than other people.

QUESTIONS

1. What was the name of the feast that the Jews kept every year?
2. What were they to remember when they kept the feast?
3. Can you tell the little story of when God's people were slaves in Egypt?
4. Did Jesus keep the feast while he was here on earth?
5. Did he tell us to keep it now?
6. Whom did Jesus send into the town to get things ready for the feast?
7. Whom did he say they would see when they entered the town?

8. Were they to follow the man into a house?

9. Did they find the man just as Jesus said they would?

10. Did they prepare the feast?

11. Why did Jesus get up from the table during the supper?

12. Did Peter want Jesus to wash his feet?

13. What had the disciples been disputing over?

14. What did Jesus say they must do to be great?

The Lord's Supper
(Matt. 26:19-30)

While Jesus and his disciples were eating the Passover feast, Jesus told them that one of them would betray him. That meant that one of them would tell the wicked rulers how they could find Jesus and kill him.

It made the disciples very sad when Jesus told them that. They began to look at one another and wonder who it could be who could be so wicked.

One after another they asked, "Lord is it I?"

Now, one of the disciples whom Jesus loved very much was leaning with his head on Jesus' breast. Peter told him to ask Jesus who it was who should betray him.

Jesus said, "It is the one who shall put his hand with me into the dish." Then Judas reached his hand in the dish with him.

Jesus turned to him and said, "What you are going to do, do quickly."

Now, the other disciples did not know what Jesus meant, but Judas knew. The devil had made Judas' heart very wicked.

Judas got up quickly and went out. He went to find the wicked rulers and tell them how they could take Jesus.

Jesus told the disciples that it would have been better if Judas had not been born.

While they were eating supper, Jesus took some bread, broke it, gave thanks to God, and gave it to his disciples.

He told them to eat it because it was his body that would be broken for them.

He took a cup, gave thanks to God, and gave to them.

He told them to drink it because it was his blood that he was going to shed for them.

He told them that he would not eat of the bread or drink of the cup any more until after his death.

He told them that they were to eat of the bread often to remember his body and to drink of the cup to remember his blood because he was giving his life for them.

We are to eat of the bread and drink of the cup on the first day of the week.

When we do we must always think about Jesus and all he has done for us.

We must also remember that he has said that he is coming back from heaven some day to take all the good people to live with him there.

After they had finished eating, Jesus told his disciples that he was going to be killed, but he would come to life again.

They were very sad, but he told them not to be sad because he was going up to heaven to prepare a place for them.

Then they all sang a song together and went out of the room into a place called the Mount of Olives. Jesus was going there to pray.

QUESTIONS

1. What did Jesus tell his disciples that one of them would do?
2. How did the disciples feel?

3. What did they ask Jesus?
4. Which one did he say it would be?
5. What did he tell Judas?
6. Did the others know what he meant?
7. Where did Judas go?
8. What did Jesus do with the bread while they were eating?
9. What did he say the bread was?
10. What did he do with the cup?
11. What did he say the cup was?
12. When are we to eat of the bread and drink of the cup?
13. What are we to think about?
14. What did Jesus begin to tell his disciples?
15. Did it make them sad?
16. Why did he say they should not be sad?
17. What did they do before they left the room?
18. Where did they go?
19. What was Jesus going to do?

Jesus in the Garden

(Matt. 26:31-46)

After Jesus and his disciples had left the place where they had eaten the supper together, they started toward a place called the Mount of Olives.

There was a garden called Gethsemane where Jesus often went to pray.

On the way he told his disciples that all of them would be offended in him that night and would leave him.

Peter said he would never do that. He was ready to die with Jesus, he thought.

Jesus said, "Before the cock crows you will deny three times that you even know me."

Peter said he would never say that he did not know Jesus. All the other disciples said the same thing.

When they reached the garden, Jesus left all but three of his disciples at the entrance. He told them to stay and watch.

He took Peter, James and John and went on into the garden.

He left them there and said, "Stay here while I go over yonder and pray."

He went away about as far as some one could throw a rock and fell down on his face and prayed.

He said, "Father, if it be thy will, let this cup pass from me. Nevertheless, not my will, but thine be done."

He was very sad, and he prayed that he might not have to suffer so much.

While he was praying an angel came

and stood by him to keep him from being so sad.

When he came back to his disciples, he found them asleep.

He said to Peter, "Could you not watch with me one hour?"

He went away the second time and prayed again.

He knew that he was to be killed and that all his friends would leave him. He was very, very sad.

He came back and found his disciples sleeping again. They did not understand all the things he had told them about his death.

He went away the third time and prayed saying the same words.

When he came back to his disciples this time he said, "Get up now and let us be going. The one who will betray me is coming. The time has come when

I am to be given to the wicked people."

While he was talking, there came into the garden a group of men with swords and staves just as if they had come to get a very wicked man.

Judas was leading the group.

QUESTIONS

1. Where did Jesus and his disciples go after they had eaten supper?
2. What was the name of the garden?
3. Did Jesus often go there? Why?
4. What did Jesus say that his disciples would all do that night?
5. What did Peter say?
6. What did Jesus say Peter would do three times?
7. How many of the disciples did Jesus leave at the entrance to the garden?
8. Whom did he take farther into the garden?
9. What did he tell them to do?
10. Where did he go to pray?
11. How many times did he pray?

12. What did he say when he prayed?
13. Who came to him while he was praying to keep him from being so sad?
14. What were the disciples doing when he came back?
15. What did he tell the disciples when he came back the third time?
16. Who was coming into the garden?
17. Who was leading the group?

Jesus Taken by Wicked People
(John 18:1-12)

Now Judas knew the place where Jesus often went with his disciples to pray. When he left the supper and went to the rulers he told them where they could find Jesus because he thought he would go to the garden.

He gathered together a band of wicked people who hated Jesus and started toward the garden. They carried lanterns to give light to show them the way because it was late in the night.

Judas gave the people a sign so they would know which one was Jesus.

He said, "It will be the one I kiss. Take him and hold him."

When they came into the garden, Ju-

das went to Jesus and said, "Hail, Master" and kissed him.

Jesus turned to him and said, "Do you betray me with a kiss?"

It was very wicked of Judas to kiss Jesus just as if he loved him when he was really just giving him to the wicked people.

Jesus said to the people, "Whom do you want?"

They said, "Jesus of Nazareth."

Jesus said, "I am he."

When he said that, they went backward and fell down on the ground.

Jesus said again, "Whom do you want?"

They said, "Jesus of Nazareth." They came to him and took hold of him. They tied his hands together.

Jesus said, "You have come out with swords and staves just as though you were going to take a robber. I have been teaching every day in the Temple, and you did not touch me."

The Old Testament had told how Jesus would be betrayed, and they were doing just the way it said, but they did not know it.

They were afraid to do anything to Jesus in the day time because they were afraid of the people. A crowd had followed him everywhere he went to listen to him preach.

When Peter saw what was happening, he drew out his sword and struck one of the men. He cut off his ear.

Jesus told Peter to put up his sword. He touched the man's ear and made it well again.

He told Peter he must not fight. He said he could call down an army of angels from heaven to fight for him if he wanted to, but he wanted to please God.

The only way he could please God was to die for the people.

The men took Jesus away to the rulers. All the disciples were afraid, and they ran away.

QUESTIONS

1. Did Judas know where Jesus often went to pray?
2. Whom did he gather together?
3. How did he tell them they could know Jesus?
4. When he came to Jesus what did he do?
5. What did Jesus say to the people?
6. What did they say?
7. When Jesus said, "I am he," what did they do?
8. Why were the people afraid to take Jesus in the daytime?
9. Had the Old Testament told just how Jesus would be betrayed?

10. Did the people know they were doing what the Bible said?

11. When Peter saw what was happening, what did he do?

12. What did Jesus do?

13. Whom did Jesus say he could call to fight for him if he wanted to?

14. When the people took Jesus, what did the disciples do?

Peter Denies Jesus
(Matt. 26:57-75; 27:3-10)

The band of people took Jesus away in the night to the home of the high priest, where the rulers were gathered together waiting for him.

Now Peter wanted to see what would happen to Jesus, but he was afraid to be seen close to him. He was afraid the people would take him, too.

He followed Jesus a long way off and came to the yard where they had taken him.

The people who were standing around in the yard had built a fire to keep themselves warm because it was cold.

Peter went to the fire and stood and warmed himself.

A servant girl came to him and said, "You were with Jesus."

Peter was afraid, and he said, "I was not. I do not know what you are saying."

After a while another one who was standing around in the yard said, "This man is also one of them that was with Jesus."

Peter became very angry. He said again, "I was not. I do not know the man."

A man who was standing near said, "You are one of this man's disciples because you talk like him."

Peter began to curse and to swear. He said, "I do not even know the man."

Just at that time he heard the cock crow. He remembered the words that Jesus had said, "Before the cock crows you will deny three times that you know me."

Jesus turned and looked at Peter.

It made Peter very sorry when he thought about what he had done.

He went out into the dark away from all the people and cried a long time.

Now after Judas had betrayed Jesus, he was sorry. He knew Jesus had not done anything wrong. He wished he had not taken the money from the rulers.

He went to the rulers again and tried to give them back the money. He said, "I have done wrong because I have given you a good man."

The rulers said, "We do not care how you feel. You can worry about that."

Judas was very unhappy. He threw down the money and went away from them. He felt so very bad that he went out and hanged himself so that he died.

The rulers said, "What shall we do with the money he left?"

They did not want to put it in the treasury in the Temple because it had been paid for Jesus.

They took it and bought a field to be used to bury people in who had no homes. The field has been called, "The field of blood."

QUESTIONS

1. Where did the people take Jesus?
2. What did Peter want to do?
3. Why did he not stay close to Jesus?

4. How did he follow him?

5. What did Peter do when he went into the yard?

6. What did the servant girl say to him?

7. What did he answer?

8. What did the second girl say?

9. Did he say again that he did not know Jesus?

10. What did the man say to him?

11. What did Peter do and say that time?

12. What had Jesus told him he would do?

13. What did Peter do when he remembered?

14. What did Judas do when he thought about the bad thing he had done?

15. Did the rulers care how he felt?

16. What did Judas do with the money?

17. What did he do when he went away?

18. What did the rulers do with the money he left?

The Death of Jesus

(Matt. 27)

The wicked rulers could not find anything wrong with Jesus, but they wanted to kill him because they hated him.

They said he did wrong because he said he was the Son of God.

They paid men to say things about him that were not true.

Now the governor, whose name was Pilate, could not find anything wrong with Jesus. He knew that the people wanted him killed just because they did not like him. He did not want to have him killed.

While he was sitting in his seat listening to the people tell wicked things about Jesus, some one came to him and said: "Your wife said for you not to have anything to do with this good man."

She had dreamed about Jesus that day, and she knew he was good. She did not want Pilate to send him to be killed.

That made Pilate more afraid. He did not want to kill Jesus, but he wanted to please the people. The people wanted him killed, so he did not know what to do.

Each year at the feast that we have been learning about, the governor brought one man out of prison and let him be free.

The people always told him whom they wanted.

Pilate picked out one of the most wicked men in the prison and asked if the people wanted the wicked man, whose name was Barabbas, or if they wanted Jesus to be free.

He thought they would say Jesus because Barabbas was so wicked, but they cried out, "Barabbas."

He said then, "What shall I do with Jesus?"

They all said, "Let him be crucified."

When they crucified a person they nailed his hands and feet to a cross and left him hanging there until he died.

Pilate was sorry, but he wanted to please the people, so he took a pan of water and washed his hands. He said,

"You can take him and do as you please. I will not have anything to do with it."

The soldiers took Jesus, beat him, spit on him, and treated him very badly.

They carried him outside the city and nailed him on the cross. They left him there to die.

They wrote on a board and put over his head, "This is Jesus, the King of the Jews."

Two other men were killed at the same time. They were thieves. They had been very wicked men.

The soldiers put one thief on one side of Jesus, and the other on the other side.

The people who stood by the cross where Jesus was, said very wicked things to him.

They said, "If you are the Son of God come down from the cross."

They said he had made sick people

well so he should be able to come down from the cross.

They did not know that he was dying to take away the sins of all the people. He was pleasing God.

It was about the middle of the day when Jesus was put on the cross.

After a little while it became dark just like night and stayed dark for three hours.

One of the soldiers said, "Surely this man must be the Son of God."

After a few hours Jesus died.

A good man whose name was Joseph came and asked Pilate if he could take

Jesus' body down from the cross and bury it.

Pilate told him he could. He and some others who loved Jesus went and took him down and buried him.

The place where they buried him was a cave cut out of the rocks. They rolled a big stone over the door when they had buried him.

Now Jesus' mother, some other women, and the disciples saw where they buried him.

They were very sad and cried because he was dead.

QUESTIONS

1. Why did the wicked rulers want to kill Jesus?
2. Why did they pay men to say bad things against him?
3. What was the governor's name?
4. Did he want to kill Jesus?

5. Did he want to please the people?

6. What did Pilate's wife say?

7. Whom did Pilate pick out in the prison to ask the people if they wanted him to be free?

8. Which one did they ask for: Jesus or Barabbas?

9. How did the soldiers treat Jesus?

10. How did they kill him?

11. Who were placed on the crosses on each side of Jesus?

12. What did they write on a board and put over Jesus' head?

13. What happened while Jesus was on the cross?

14. What did one of the soldiers say?

15. Who came and asked to bury Jesus?

16. Where did they bury him?

17. How did the women and the disciples feel?

The Resurrection
(Matt. 27:62-66; Mk. 16:1-8; John 20:1-10)

Now when Jesus was dead and had been buried, the wicked rulers went to Pilate. They asked him to put soldiers at the tomb to watch.

They remembered that when Jesus was alive he told them that he would be killed but he would come back alive in three days.

They did not believe that he could come back alive. They said they were afraid his disciples would go and steal his body out of the grave and say that he had risen from the dead.

Pilate sent some soldiers to watch the tomb.

Very early on the first day of the week, or Sunday as we now call it, some of the women who loved Jesus came to the grave where he was buried.

They wanted to put some spices on his body just as they fixed other people when they died.

As they were going along the way they began to say one to another, "Who will roll away the stone from the door for us?"

There had been a very large stone placed over the entrance to the cave. The women were not strong enough to roll it away, so they were wondering about it as they went along.

They were very sad because Jesus was dead.

When they came to the tomb, they saw a strange thing. The large stone was rolled away, and Jesus was gone out of the grave.

They were frightened and could not imagine what had happened.

They went into the tomb. There they saw a young man dressed in white sitting on the right side of the tomb.

They were more afraid, but the young man, who was really an angel, said to them, "Do not be afraid. You are looking for Jesus. He is not here. He has come back from the dead. Do you not remember that he told you before he died that he would come back to life again in three days?"

He told them to go and tell his disciples, especially Peter, that Jesus was alive again and that they would soon get to see him.

The women hardly knew what to say. They could hardly believe that Jesus was alive.

They did not know that an angel had come while it was dark and rolled the large stone away and Jesus had come out of the grave alive again.

They hurried away to tell the disciples what they had seen. They told Peter and John first, and they could hardly believe what they heard.

They started running to the tomb.

John ran faster than Peter and came to the tomb first. He stooped down and looked in, but he did not go in.

After a while Peter came, and he went into the tomb.

After he had gone in, John went in, too.

They saw the clothes that had been around Jesus' body folded neatly lying in the grave. The cloth that had been around Jesus' head was folded and lying by itself in another place.

When they saw these things they believed that Jesus had come back from the dead.

They left the tomb and went away to their own homes wondering about the things they had seen.

QUESTIONS

1. What did the wicked rulers ask Pilate to do?
2. What had Jesus said he would do?
3. Did the rulers believe he would rise from the dead?
4. When did the women come to the tomb?
5. What were they going to do?
6. What did they ask each other on the way?
7. What strange thing did they see when they came to the tomb?
8. Whom did they see in the grave?

9. What did the angel say to them?
10. Whom did he tell them to go and tell?
11. Whom did they first tell?
12. What did Peter and John do?
13. Which one came to the tomb first?
14. Who went into the tomb first?
15. What did they see in the tomb?
16. Did they believe that Jesus had risen from the dead?

Mary Magdalene Sees Jesus
Two Disciples See Him

(John 20:11-18; Lk. 24:13-31)

Mary Magdalene was one of the women who had loved Jesus while he was alive. She was very sad when he was killed.

She came to the tomb on the first day of the week just as the other women did.

She was standing outside the tomb weeping because Jesus was gone and she did not know where he was.

While she was crying, she stooped down and looked into the grave. There she saw two angels, one sitting at the head and the other at the foot.

They said to her, "Why are you weeping?"

She answered, "Because they have taken away my Lord, and I do not know where they have laid him."

Just as she said that she turned around and saw Jesus standing by her.

She did not know that it was Jesus. She thought it was the man who took care of the garden.

Jesus said to her, "Why are you weeping? Whom are you looking for?"

She said, "If you have taken him away, tell me where you have put him, and I will take him away from there."

Jesus said to her, "Mary." When he said her name she knew that it was Jesus.

She was very happy. Jesus told her not to touch him then but to go and tell his disciples that she had seen him. She ran quickly and told them that Jesus was alive again and that she had seen him.

Now two of Jesus' disciples were going that very day to a little town called Emmaus, which was not far from Jerusalem.

As they were walking along they were talking about Jesus. They could not understand all the things they had heard that day about him.

Jesus came near them and walked along with them, but they did not know it was Jesus.

He asked them what they were talking about. They stopped walking and stood still. They looked very sad. They were surprised that there was any one who did not know about all the things that had been happening.

He asked them, "What things?"

They began to tell him all about Jesus, how great a teacher he was and how he could heal the sick, raise the dead, and make blind people see. They told how the wicked rulers had hated him and had put him to death.

They said it had been three days since he died and some of the women had been to the tomb and had come away saying that he had risen from the dead.

Jesus began to teach them what the prophets and others had said who had written about him. He told them that God had planned to send his Son into the world to die for the people.

When they came to the house where the disciples were going, they asked Jesus to come into their house and spend the night because it was late in the day. They still did not know that it was Jesus.

He went into their house and sat down with them to eat supper. He took some bread and looked up to God and gave thanks for it.

While he was praying they discovered that it was Jesus.

Suddenly he disappeared out of their sight. They could not see him any more.

They got up from the table right away and went back to Jerusalem to tell the other disciples that they had seen Jesus.

QUESTIONS

1. What was Mary Magdalene doing as she was standing by the tomb?
2. Whom did she see in the tomb?
3. What did the angels say to her?
4. Why did she say she was weeping?
5. When she turned around whom did she see?
6. Who did she think it was?
7. What did Jesus say to her?
8. What did she say?
9. What did he say that made her know who it was?

10. Whom did he tell her to go tell?
11. When the two disciples were going to Emmaus who came and walked with them?
12. Did they know him?
13. What did he ask them?
14. What did they tell him?
15. Did he tell them what the prophets had written about him?
16. When they got to the house where they were going, what did they ask Jesus to do?
17. When did they know him?
18. What did they do right away?

All the Disciples See Jesus

(Luke 24:36-48; John 20:24-29)

As soon as the two men reached Jerusalem they went into the house where Jesus' disciples were gathered together.

The disciples were afraid of the Jews because they thought the Jews might try to kill them. They had the doors locked.

The two men began to tell them that they had seen Jesus and how they knew him when he blessed the bread while they were eating.

The disciples said that Peter had seen him, too. They were wondering about all the things they had heard.

Suddenly while they were talking, they saw Jesus standing in the middle of the room. They were all afraid and thought they saw a spirit.

Jesus spoke to them and told them not to be afraid. He showed them his hands and his feet where the prints of the nails were so they would know that it was really he.

Still they could not believe it was he because they were so happy.

He said to them, "Do you have anything to eat?"

They gave him a piece of cooked fish, and he ate it before them. They knew then that it was really Jesus. They were so happy to see him and hear him talk again.

He scolded them because they had not believed him at first. He began to teach them again the things that the prophets had written about him. They believed those things now since they had seen him alive again.

Now one of the disciples, named Thomas, was not with them when Jesus came, so he did not see him.

The other disciples told him, "We have seen Jesus."

He did not believe them.

He said he would not believe Jesus was alive unless he could put his fingers in the prints of the nails in his hands and put his hand in his side where the print of the sword was.

Eight days later the disciples were together again in a room with the doors locked. Thomas was with them.

Suddenly they saw Jesus standing by them just as they had seen him before.

He went to Thomas and showed him his hands where the nails had been driven and showed him his side where the sword had been put. He asked Thomas to believe on him and not to say any more that he did not believe.

Thomas said, "My Lord and my God."

Jesus said, "You believe on me because you have seen me. Blessed are those people who have not seen me and yet believe on me."

QUESTIONS

1. Where were the disciples gathered together?
2. Why did they have the doors locked?
3. While they were talking, whom did they see standing in the room?
4. How did they feel?
5. What did Jesus show them?
6. What did he ask them?
7. What did they give him to eat?
8. Were all the disciples there?
9. Which one was not there?

10. What did Thomas say when they told him they had seen Jesus?

11. Eight days later was Thomas with the disciples when Jesus came?

12. What did Jesus tell Thomas to do?

13. What did Thomas say to Jesus?

14. Did Jesus say that people would be blessed who have not seen him and yet believe on him?

Jesus Goes to Heaven

(Mark 16:14-20; Acts 1:1-12)

After Jesus arose from the dead, he stayed on the earth for forty days.

He did not stay with his disciples all the time, but he appeared to them several times. He talked to them about the work they were to do after he went back to heaven.

One day he let more than five hundred people see him at one time.

One day he came to his disciples and told them that God had given him all power in heaven and on earth.

He told them to go into all the world and teach about him to everybody in the world.

He said that everybody who believes in him and is baptized will be saved, but everybody who does not believe in him will be lost.

He led his disciples out of the city of Jerusalem to the Mount of Olives near to the little town of Bethany, and there he talked with them.

While he was talking he was taken up in the sky. A cloud hid him so that the disciples could not see him.

They stood there gazing up into heaven wondering about what they had seen.

Two men suddenly stood by them. They were angels and were dressed all in white.

The angels said, "Why are you standing here looking up into heaven?"

They told the disciples that Jesus had gone up to heaven to live with God. They said that some day he will come back just as they saw him leave.

When he comes back he will come to

take all the good people up to heaven to live with him.

The disciples left the mountain and went back to Jerusalem, just as Jesus had told them to do.

He told them to wait in the city of Jerusalem until he sent the Holy Spirit to them. When the Holy Spirit came to them, he was to help them remember all the things Jesus had done and taught. Then they would be ready to go into all the world and teach about Jesus.

QUESTIONS

1. How long did Jesus stay on the earth after he rose from the dead?
2. Did he stay with the disciples all the time?
3. How many people saw him at one time?
4. Where did Jesus tell his disciples they were to go to preach?
5. To whom were they to preach?

6. Who will be saved?

7. Who will be lost?

8. Where did he lead his disciples one day?

9. While he was talking to them what happened?

10. While they were gazing into heaven, who stood by them?

11. What did the angels tell them?

12. Where did the disciples go?

13. Whom had Jesus promised to send to them?

14. What was the Holy Spirit going to help them do?

15. Would they be ready then to preach to everybody about Jesus?